MORE OF THE FUNNIEST MAN IN THE WORLD

MORE OF THE FUNNIEST MAN IN THE WORLD

THE WILD AND CRAZY HUMOR OF

EPHRAIM KISHON

SHAPOLSKY PUBLISHERS, INC.

Published in the United States of America 1989 by
Shapolsky Publishers, Inc.

First published in the United Kingdom 1989 by
PRION, an imprint of Multimedia Books Limited,
32/34 Gordon House Road, London NW5 1LP

Translated from the Hebrew by Johanan Goldman and Miriam Arad
Cover illustration by Itzik Rennert

For any additional information, contact:

Shapolsky Publishers, Inc.
136 West 22nd Street, New York, NY 10011
212–633–2022

9 8 7 6 5 4 3 2 1

Library of Congress Cataloging-in-Publication Data

Kishon, Ephraim
More of the Funniest Man in the World:
The Wild and Crazy Humor of Ephraim Kishon
1. Wit and humor. 2. Ephraim Kishon.
ISBN 0-944007-48-1

Typeset by Wyvern Typesetting Limited, UK
Jacket origination by Reprocraft 87 Limited, UK
Printed in the United Kingdom by The Bath Press Limited

CONTENTS

☐ The Jew's crooked mind, the anti-Semites claim, never rests. We are credited with many brilliant inventions, no one can deny it. I would like to present here a list of the latest, as proof that the time has come to take a brief rest.

EXERCISE AT 3:45

———————☐———————

We were sitting, Ervinke[1] and me, staring at the demitasses in front of us. The time was 3:45, naturally P.M., and it was hanging like a dead weight on our minds. In the distance, Dizengoff Street was flowing raucously. A velocity-12 *khamsin* was blowing and the mailmen had been on strike for the past two weeks. Nothing. The boredom was even worse than usual.

"Listen," Ervinke finally muttered, "why don't they design cups for southpawed folks – that is, with the handle on the other side of the cup?"

"Do you think they care? Don't you know them? Sales is all they care about."

"For five thousand years the same boring cups," Ervinke sighed. "Did they ever try to place the handle inside, so as not to disrupt the cup's outer wholeness?"

"Never," I replied. "Everything they do is routine."

Ervinke raised the conventional cup to his lips and sipped.

"Just a little thought," he went on, "just a little attention to details! Take pins. All over the world at least a hundred thousand people are getting pinpricks every hour. If they'd only manufacture

---

[1] Ervinke is not a Jewish name at all. To spare the reader the trouble of remembering tongue-twisting genuine Hebrew names, we decided to use names more familiar to the average civilized person. Ervinke's genuine Israel name would be Elyakim. Or take the present author: he started out in life as Francis, but is now better known as Ephraim.

pins with heads on both ends, nobody would prick himself."

"Absolutely," I said. "That's just like toothless combs for baldheads."

"I beg your pardon, but that's infantile."

I fell silent. When I am insulted I clam up.

"This is no time for foolishness," Ervinke chided me. "I am discussing practical things. Like plastic dandruff. It's just come out. You scatter a little on your hair and that's that."

"It will never look genuine."

"No? You can look at it through a lens and you will never know the difference! We are living in an age of new materials, old boy. Ever seen a glass hat?"

"No," I admitted. "Why glass?"

"If you drop it, you don't have to bend down and pick it up."

That sounded logical. It looked as if mankind was, after all, not marking time.

"What would you think of a cupboard," I asked, "with four legs on top as well?"

Ervinke looked at me, surprised. He always thinks I'm not too bright.

"Legs on top?" he mused. "I see: if the top gets dusty, you simply turn the cupboard upside down."

"Obvious."

"These household things are very practical," said Ervinke. "Take round handkerchiefs. I have been trying to get some for years."

"You don't have to fold them, eh?"

"Right."

"I've got something like that myself," I confessed, blushing. "I've even thought of taking out a patent on it."

"Well?"

"A trousers traffic light. A miniature electronic instrument for the benefit of the well-dressed gentleman. If a button opens in your fly, a red light flashes and a buzzer sounds."

Ervinke blinked, greatly perplexed. He had not credited me with such perspicacity.

"Your traffic light is too complicated," he said in a voice hollow with envy. "It reminds me of the professor's cuckoo trap. You install it in front of the door of the cuckoo clock and when the bird comes out to blare its unnerving cuckoo, a small hammer hits it over the head and silences it forever."

"How many people in this country have cuckoo clocks?"

"Don't worry, there are plenty!"

There, now he is upset. I am sorry, but the whole idea of the cuckoo trap sounds silly from my end. If you don't want to hear the cuckoo, why not simply take the clock to a watchmaker and have him remove the bird? Why a trap? The ideas some people get.

"Did you hear about the invention of the agronomist Michurin?" I asked Ervinke. "Cross-breeding watermelons with fleas. . . ."

"So that the seeds pop out by themselves. A hoary old joke. Personally, I am more impressed by the cross-breeding of corn with a typewriter: while chewing the corn, as you reach the edge of the cob, it rings and jumps back and you can start on a new row."

"Not bad."

"Everything for comfort," Ervinke shrugged. "I read somewhere that in the U.S. they have an advanced combine which plants potatoes all by itself, then automatically sprinkles them, cultivates them, picks them, washes them, peels them, cooks them and eats them."

"Yes," I said, smiling sadly. "Man becomes superfluous. They've invented a computer in Japan which plays chess like a Grand Master."

"I'd buy two," Ervinke said, "so they'd play chess at home while I could go to the movies."

I paid and we went to the second show. Outside, an old beggar crouched, playing his transistor radio. The earth abideth forever. There is nothing new under the sun.

□ *Ervinke, myself, and the reader as well, depend to a large extent on that stubby index finger that will press the button just for the fun of it and turn all of us into blithe radioactive clouds. A somewhat tense situation, admittedly, but it has its compensations.*

A FALSE ALARM

———□———

About two weeks ago I ran into Ervinke on Dizengoff Street. My friend was sitting in our café, reading a newspaper perhaps for the first time since the creation of the State. He looked utterly dejected and his fingers beat a nervous rat-tat-tat on the tabletop.

"Money?" I inquired. "Or reluctant debutantes?"

"Peace."

"What?"

"You wanted to know what's eating me. Well, I'm telling you. It's peace."

I paid his bill, we rose and started walking up and down garishly lit Dizengoff Street. It was a pleasant spring evening. Tired spectators were just coming out of the cinemas, the sidewalks were crowded with hip-swinging females.

"Let's face it," Ervinke opened. "I'm a beatnik."

"So it seems."

"But not an amateur beatnik who drifts with the tide. Ever since I started thinking, I realized with absolute certainty that there was absolutely no certainty in my life. And that has always been a wonderful feeling! Our forefathers always had to worry about their families, about what would happen to them in their old age, how much pension they would draw, and so on. Whereas we feel as free as the birds! What's going to happen thirty years from now, you ask me? Man, I don't give a damn what's going to happen next week."

Gyuri ran past.

"After the show, at Putzi's," he threw at Ervinke. "Bring a bottle and at least one girl!"

"Sorry," Ervinke replied, "I have to get up at ten-thirty tomorrow."

"Don't get up ever," Gyuri quipped and disappeared in the crowd. Ervinke did not look offended.

"I'm invited to another party," he explained, an expectant glint in his eye. "To belong to the lost generation means you are part of a worldwide movement! Once upon a time, a square my age would have said, 'Pleasures all day long, parties every night. Where is that going to lead, how is it going to end?' But we are the lost generation, man, who knows that it's going to end in one big flash once the atom bombs start falling."

"And if not?"

"That will be just too bad. But at least you can hope that the whole world will perish, see? Without that hope, life is not worth living. If I have to worry about tomorrow, plan for when I'll be a toothless old fool, I'll go nuts, man, nuts. That only makes life complicated, believe me. Once upon a time the squares had to whisper in a girl's ears about chubby babies, a little white house and all that before they could get anything out of them. Nowadays we fix these things easily and smoothly. 'What do you care? Who knows what's going to happen tomorrow?' See what I mean?"

A taxi driver started blowing his horn because we were crossing while the light was amber.

"Where are your eyes, stupid?" Ervinke roared and kicked a mudguard viciously. "Can't you see you have the right of way?"

The driver blinked his eyes in confusion and mumbled something about traffic laws according to which he had the right of way. Ervinke put his hand through the window and ruffled the driver's hair playfully.

"Laws?" he said. "Man, Libya's going to have nuclear weapons next year! Laws, he says! Get going!"

Suddenly Ervinke stopped and his brown eyes darkened.

"Last night I woke with a start and the terrible thought occurred to me that, who knows, they might make peace all over the world, rashly destroy all atomic weapons, and then I, a lone beatnik, will be left here in the middle of Dizengoff Street without any moral foundation, without a profession, without anything except a long-play future. It's a real nightmare!"

"Things aren't as bad as all that."

"Aw, leave me alone!" Ervinke fumed. "They're pulling the rug out from under me. I can't stand the thought of it. Suddenly to have to grow up, to sweat for a lousy salary, to have children and a paunch, to put your savings in a bank at three and three-quarters percent interest! Horrible! In the buses they'll give their seats to elderly people, they'll read fat books and sleep at night, Clothes will be painfully well pressed, buses will run on time and the girls will be good. Ghastly!"

Shuddering, Ervinke kicked a garbage can, sending it flying through space.

"It's easy for some hotheads to rave about disarmament," he said, "but who will be responsible for the consequences?"

GOING DUTCH

———————□———————

   "I've been had," said Ervinke. "Boy, have I been had!"
We were sitting in Gusti's, and as this looked like becoming a long story, I ordered us two instants and settled down to listen.

"I met this chick about a fortnight ago," said my friend, nervously fiddling with his spoon. "Libby was her name. She seemed to like me too, and we started going out together. She respected the pragmatist in me, whereas I admired her legs and her taste in earrings. Everything was coming along fine, until the evening we decided to go on a spree. . . ."

Ervinke heaved a deep sigh.

"I suggested coffee and cake for a start, then a show, then a real smashing dinner to round it off. 'Very well, Ervinke,' said Libby, 'but I won't have you pay for me. I'm a modern girl!' I told her it was beneath my dignity to keep account of every piddling expense and then charge her half, so Libby said: 'All right, Ervinke, tell you what we'll do: we'll take turns paying . . .'

"Well, that's how it started. We met at the bus stop and took a bus to this café. When we get on the bus Libby says: 'Ladies first, Ervinke, the tickets are on me!' and she buys two tickets at two shekels' each. Then we get to this café, where we put away six chocolate-and-almond cakes and coffee with cream, and I paid Sh.42·50, because now it was *my* turn. . . .

"Next we took a bus to the theater," Ervinke continued with a frown. "Libby paid the fare again, informing me over her shoulder that a girl has her principles, and she for one meant to stick by hers. Then *I* bought the tickets for the show at Sh.48, since she only sees properly from the front row, and she paid the cloakroom attendant 50 agorot, as per agreement.

'In Israel we buy, sell and negotiate in shekels. For small change we use agorot. Sh.1 = 100 agorot.

"The show itself wasn't bad, though my mind kept wandering because the way I figured it – *I* would pay for the ride to the restaurant now, and *she* would pay for the food, which would make all the difference. . . ."

At this point Ervinke asked Gusti for a glass of water and gulped it in one go.

"After the first act, Libby suggested we stretch our legs a bit in the foyer. I said 'Why, darling, we're sitting all nice and snug here,' but she insisted. Out there she went straight to the counter and treated herself to a cheese sandwich. 'Mm,' she said, munching happily. 'Delicious. It's your turn, Ervinke.'

"I could hear alarm bells ringing in my head, because now *Libby* would pay for the bus and *I* for the food, dammit. So I waited quietly through the interval, and at the last moment turned to Libby and said: 'How about a glass of soda?' She didn't feel thirsty, somehow, but me – I was parched! 'Pay up, sweetheart – 2 shekels,' I nudged her, and she paid up like a man!

"That's how it happened that all through the second act it was my turn for bus tickets again. In the interval I refused to budge, pleading lumbago. Libby gave me a long look out of her brown eyes, then said: 'Of course. Just call the ice cream boy. . . .' meaning some brat running up and down the aisle with his tray, they shouldn't allow it. In short, I bought her her bloody ice cream, and as a result I've no idea what the third act was about, since my mind was searching frantically for a way out.

"When we rose at the end I turned the discussion on the actors. 'Know what?' I told Libby, 'Let's buy a program!' A fleeting shadow crossed my Libby's face: 'Now?' she said, '*After* the show? . . .Oh, all right, Ervinke, I'll buy one.' And did. And paid."

Ervinke's lips twisted in a peculiar smile.

"When I bought the bus tickets," he resumed, "I still felt on top of the world. And at the restaurant I really let myself go. I ordered a clear consommé, followed by veal *à la dauphinoise* with asparagus, and salad, and coffee and strudel and pineapple. Libby just sat staring rather desperately at my plate and hardly touched her food. In the end I ordered a cigar although I don't smoke – and asked for the check. Libby closed her eyes and took a deep breath . . . and then, right then, this louse entered the restaurant. . . ."

Ervinke asked for another glass of water.

"The louse came in and started peddling shoelaces. I ask you! Shoelaces! In the middle of the night! I was quite ready to wring his neck, but I didn't dare move for fear of drawing Libby's attention to the wretch. . . . 'The check! Quick!' I yelled at the waiter, and then what do you suppose happened? The louse heard me yelling and came right over! I sent him unmistakable go-to-hell signals – but in vain. . . ."

Ervinke groaned.

"Libby bought a pair of black laces at 80 agorot, and I slapped down Sh.158 plus service for the feast. And then of course she paid the bus fare home again, fair is fair. . . . And that isn't all! When we got to her door at last and I wanted to kiss her good night, she pushed me away firmly and said: 'See, Ervinke, *that's* why I didn't want you to pay for me!'

"That . . ." Ervinke sobbed, "you hear . . . that's why she didn't . . . she didn't . . . want me . . . to pay. . . ."

☐ *The stomach is like most trade unions: it does not take orders from anybody, but goes its own narrow-minded way.*

This causes a great many complications.

The new immigrant to Israel gets off the boat, kisses the ground his ancestors trod, smashes a few government office windows, settles down in the Negev, and then becomes a fully integrated Israeli citizen. But his conservative and prejudiced stomach stays Hungarian, Turkish, Dutch, or whatever the case may be.

SHASHLIK, SUM-SUM, WUS-WUS

———— ☐ ————

Take myself, to be more specific. I have become an old-timer to the extent that I even affect a slight Russian accent, and yet even now I scream in my sleep when I remember that for the past seven years I have not once eaten stuffed goose liver.

In the beginning I fought this cosmopolitan attitude. I told Stomach with as much conviction in my voice as I could muster: "Stuffed goose liver is phooey! We'll eat a lot of nice black olives, my boy, and become as strong as the village bull at harvest time."

But Stomach countered this with (I'm blushing, really) "Go to hell!" and insisted on an overcivilized diet.[1]

---

[1] My obstinately Hungarian stomach is causing me no end of trouble. In the United States they once almost lynched me because of it.

It happened at a cafeteria as I was advancing with my loaded tray and reached the sign "Iced Tea." I said to the waitress behind the counter, "Glass of cold tea, without ice."

"Yes, sir," the waitress answered, and dropped half a dozen ice cubes into my tea.

"Look here," I said. "I told you 'without ice.'"

For a while I kept my stomach happy by favoring a decadently European restaurant, and it was satisfied. But then I moved to a new

"You want iced tea, mister?"

"I want cold tea."

The girl blinked like a fogbound semaphore, then, somewhat puzzled, dropped a few more ice cubes into my tea.

"There you are. Next!"

"Just the contrary, sister, I want it without ice."

"You can't have it without ice. Next!"

"Why can't I?"

"The ice is free. Next!"

"But ice makes my stomach ache. Why can't you give me a glass of tea just as it is, without putting ice in it?"

"What? How?" she spluttered. "I don't get you, mister."

The people in line behind me started muttering about foreign idiots who waste the public's valuable time. I took the hint, but at the same time the Oriental's famous pride rose in me.

"Still, I want it without ice."

The waitress realized that she had done her duty, so she called out the manager, a cigar-chewing giant.

"Man here wants iced tea without ice," the waitress complained. "Whoever heard of such a thing?"

"My dear sir," – the manager turned to me – "every month, 1,930,000 guests drink our iced tea, and there have never yet been any complaints."

"I'm sure there weren't," I replied. "But I don't like my drinks too cold; that's why I want it without ice."

"But everybody takes it with ice!"

"I don't."

The manager looked at me, frowning.

"What do you mean, you don't? What's good for a 160 million Americans isn't good enough for you?"

"Ice gives me stomach ache."

The manager laid his brows in deep furrows, trying to figure it all out, but obviously my request did not make sense to him.

"This place has been open for business for the past forty-three years," he informed me, "and up to now we have served 23 million people."

"I don't want it with ice!"

By then, the frustrated diners had encircled me and were rolling up their sleeves for the lynching. The manager decided that the time was ripe for losing his temper.

"In America you drink your tea with ice!" he roared. "I've never yet met a more stubborn crank in all my life!"

"I only . . ."

"I know your kind. Nothing is good enough for you. Where are you from?"

"Who, me?" I asked. "from Egypt."

"Just as I thought," said the manager.

19

neighborhood in which there was only one small café, managed by a certain Naftali, newly arrived from Iraq.[2]

The first time I dropped in at Naftali's, Stomach began prancing as he does only in times of mortal danger. Naftali stood behind the counter surveying me, the Mona Lisa's mysterious smile on his lips, while the counter itself was lined with a variety of nondescript raw materials in technicolor, and on a shelf in the background small cans with amusing spices were kept in readiness.

There was no doubt whatsoever that I had stumbled on an outspokenly Arab-language eating place, but before I could beat a hasty retreat, Stomach signaled that he was in a hurry.

"Well, what can I have today?" I asked in a firm voice, whereupon Naftali looked at a point about five inches to the right of my head (he is slightly cross-eyed) and said: 'I have *humus*, or *mehshi* with *burgul*, or *wus-wus*."

The choice was a difficult one. The *humus* faintly reminded me of some Latin quotation, but the *wus-wus* completely baffled me.

"Give me a platter of *wus-wus*," I threw at Naftali, whereupon he placed a fantastic potpourri of eggplant, rice, and ground meat on my plate. Its taste was extremely queer, but I wanted to prove to Naftali that his mysterious smile was lost on me. Not only that, but to make his defeat complete, I lightly threw at him somewhat later: "Got anything else?"

"Yes, sir," Naftali replied, grinning disrespectfully. "I also have *kebab* with *beharat*, *shashlik* with *elfa*, and perhaps a cut of *wehon* or *smir-smir*."

"All right," I said. "Give me a bit of everything."

I ordered in this vague way because I simply could not remember

Then I had to run for my life, with the irate crowd in hot pursuit. But that was only the beginning. Wherever I went, American public opinion was slowly turning against Egypt.

[2]Iraq expelled about 200,000 Jews, hoping they would lower Israel's living standard to her own. This plan misfired. The Iraqi Jews were completely integrated into the country's economic life, but after partaking of their cooking, one has to summon the fire brigade.

the exotic names. I expected Naftali to serve some highly seasoned cakes, or a gluey compote, or some such fodder. Instead he stepped into a secluded recess and started grinding a slab of red meat and sprinkled on it pepper and oil, and pollen, and sulphuric acid from a green phial. . . .

Two weeks later, the doctors let me get out of bed and back to work. I was rather weak in the knees, but otherwise felt fairly well, for the memory of the banquet had receded into the dim past. And then, what does blind fate decree?

As I walked toward the office, Naftali came out of his poison den and tittered behind my back. Now, I am inordinately proud and quickly lose my temper. I went straight in, looked Naftali straight in the eyes, and said: "Something nice and strong, *habibi!*"

"Right!" Naftali reacted. "I have today some first-class *kiba* with *kamon*, or *hashi-hashi.*"

I ordered a double portion of what proved to be an archaeological find incorporating all the known flavorings from *falafel* to fried onion, plus a dash of stewed emery powder. I worked through it all and then clamored for dessert.

"*Suarsi* with *mish-mish*, or *baklava* with *sum-sum?*"

I ate both. Two days later I could no longer feel a thing. And at the week's end I turned in like a sleepwalker at smiling Naftali's. To this day I don't know why I did this. Perhaps I ought to consult a good psychiatrist.

"And what would you like today, sir?" Naftali asked, contempt of the European weakling unconcealed on his face.

I found this extremely mean on his part. Why does he have to pull my leg? Does he not know that I have no idea what his outlandish dishes are called?

"Give me a *kimsu*," I desperately improvised. "And a piece of *sbaghi* with *kub-kubon.*"

And then what do you think happened?

Naftali politely said, "All right," and brought me ground mutton with mashed turnips.

You could have knocked me down with a feather. "What's going on here?" I thought.

"Hey!" I roared at Naftali. "Where's that *kub-kubon?*"

I am still trembling when I think of it: Naftali jumped and brought me the *kub-kubon* in a small box.

"You know what ?" I turned to Naftali at the end of the meal. "Bring me a glass of *vago-giora*,[3] but make sure it is ice-cold!"

I quaffed the *vago-giora* and slowly the truth dawned on me. *"Burgul, baharat, shashslik, wus-wus, mehsi, pehsi"* were all just one big fraud to awe the silly Ashkenazim.[4] So that is the secret of the Mona Lisa's smile?

Since then, I am no longer afraid of Oriental cooking; in fact, it is rather the other way around. Yesterday I even made a red-faced Naftali take back a plate of roasted *mao-mao.*

"You call this *mao-mao?*" I jeered. "Where is the *kafka?*"

And I wouldn't touch the *mao-mao* until Naftali, trembling all over, brought me a tumbler of *kafka.*[5] It tasted rather nice. I warmly advise the reader to drop in someday at an Oriental restaurant and order roasted *mao-mao* with a drop of *kafka.* If they have run out of *kafka, saroyan* will also do. Take my word for it.

[3]Vago Giora is the name of a bank manager acquaintance of ours. Once he arranged us a fairly large loan, and we thought it fitting to immortalize his name.

[4]European Jews are called by the non-European Jews "Ashkenazim" or "wus-wus" in imitation of the sound of the Yiddish language.

[5]Franz Kafka's literary merits are perhaps debatable, but with curry sauce he tastes wonderful.

DEVIL'S BROTH

————□————

I love soup.

Maybe this gastronomic predilection doesn't exactly affect the shape of modern society, but it does carry some weight on the personal plane. Mankind is split into two rival camps: those who eat soup before the main course and those who skip it altogether. There exists a Third Party too: those for whom soup *is* the main course. Myself, I belong to this small but fanatic caste. For me, a noble consommé complete with golden rings on top is sheer poetry, and a hefty matso ball is an inspirational object. "Anyone who loves soup can't be all bad," as someone said – Mark Twain was it?

However, there is a snag: soup is hot. Soup is always too hot.

This is a conclusion reached after a lifetime of experience and souplore. We have yet to encounter – in restaurants, private homes or other soup-dispensing establishments – any kind of pottage that won't give us blisters. It always causes us great mental anguish too, because the soup is there, it lies bodily in front of our nose, its fragrance sends tremors of delight through our frame, our stomach juices react with morbid lust, but we cannot touch it because it is as hot as hell.

Soup, soup, everywhere, nor any drop to drink.

We came up against this painful problem for the first time at the age of three with a fiery tomato soup which burnt our lips. Mother then introduced us to the ancient ceremonial of blowing and stirring, and I have been blowing and stirring ever since. I have been known to stir my soup and stir it until I forgot Jerusalem and my right hand withered. Once, in the city of Kiskunfelegyhàza, if memory serves me, I stirred my fabulous goulash soup into a solid mass and the spoon got stuck in it for good. These are childhood memories. Because of soup, I was a nervous and introverted kid. All my life I have longed for a little coolth. I used to look at the wide world with my big childish eyes and ask: "Why?"

I don't think there is an answer to that question even today. People have become as used to volcanic soup as they have to the lousy climate and the high taxes, and they keep stirring it absent-mindedly, as if saying: what else can we do? Very sad. At a conservative estimate, the average man spends about a year of his life cooling soups, a loss of millions of man-hours to the national economy.

Once – I'll never forget it! – at a small Italian restaurant they served me a *minestrone* which could be eaten on the spot. Either it was just not too hot, or the shredded *parmigiano* had cooled it miraculously. I don't know and I don't care. Anyway, I had two spoonfuls of it and then the *maître d'* jumped on me and snatched the plate away.

"They forgot to warm it in the kitchen," he said. I fought a desperate rearguard action against him, but he subdued me with a few well-aimed chops. When he brought the soup back I couldn't see his face for the steam. The plate burnt to a cinder on the plain deal table.

It's the same at home. If a fly wings over my wife's soup, it plummets into it like Icarus when he got too near the sun. I frequently feel the heat of the mushroom soup radiating on my calves through the table. According to elementary physics, water boils at 100 degrees centigrade, but the little one's potato soup easily rises to 140–150. Should the kind reader ever spot people walking around with swollen lips or crooked mouths, he may safely bet that they have been recent guests at our table. Once an uncle on my father's side spilled some of our soup on his chest. The doctors fought for his life for a whole week. In the end he just made it. Asparagus it was.

I implore the little woman on my knees: "Please, why so hot?"

"Don't know," she replies and gazes into the distance, "Soup's got to be hot. Stir . . . ."

There's some terrible secret about it all that nobody tells me. I visualize prehistoric man rubbing two wooden sticks together for hours on end and discovering fire. He groans, seized by superstitious fear: "S-o-u-p, s-o-u-p!" Personally, I don't give up; I carry on an obstinate and losing war against public opinion. At the restaurant, I spell it out to the waiter, stressing every syllable: *not* hot, *not* boiling, please! The waiter reacts with a glassy stare. When the kitchen door next opens, a pillar of fire leads the way.

"But I asked you," I whisper, "not to make it hot."

"You call *this* hot?" the man's voice comes out of the clouds. "This is *hot?*"

I ask him to put his finger in it. He refuses and avoids serious injury.

One day, so help me, I'll burst into the restaurant kitchen, pistol in hand: "All cooks line up against the wall! Hands up!" And then I'll turn off the flame under the chicken soup and lap it up, plate after plate – lukewarm!

Of late I have taken to ordering soup with ice cubes. Or else I carefully dribble mineral water or beer into the conflagration. Naturally it's no longer soup, but a colored liquid of doubtful meaning. But at least it's not hot.

And so I get older, and the lines on my tired face grow deeper and deeper, spelling frustration. A man who has achieved everything in life except soup that isn't hot.

On my tombstone they will carve in gilded letters: "Here lies E.K., the writer (1924–2013). Most of his life he blew and stirred."

Our forefathers who invented the Hebrew script thousands of years ago were not only southpawed and wrote from right to left but also wanted to bar the riffraff from reading the Sacred Writings, and to that end took out the vowels, the way it's done in shorthand. Therefore, it is easier to write Hebrew than to read it. Small wonder, then, that contemporary Hebrew writers are feverishly looking for readers. They have a captive audience of three – the publisher, the typesetter and the proofreader. As the fourth, they want me.

How to Review Books Without Really Trying

———□———

That thing of Tola'at Shani's worries me no end. I feel like a heel. He sent me his new book about half a year ago. I put it up on some shelf or other, and ever since it has been gathering dust and cobwebs. At first I could still think of pretexts.

"I got it," I shouted at Tola'at Shani in the street. "As soon as I get a little time, I'll read it."

The promising writer blinked gratefully. A few weeks later I again bumped into him.

"I'm reading it," I informed him falsely. "Afterward we'll talk it over!"

Afterward happened in the café. He came in, I quickly slipped out through the kitchen and I am sure he saw me. I clearly remember that on that day I made up my mind to leaf through the book carefully and, if I am not mistaken, I even stretched out my hands toward it, but just then the phone rang, or I had a seizure or something – I don't remember exactly – but anyway my hand did not touch that book. Last week Tola'at Shani grabbed me in the line at the cinema.

"Well, have you read it?" he asked anxiously, and I nodded my head mutely.

"I've got a lot to tell you," I told him, "but not standing on one foot."

And then, yesterday, he ran me down on Dizengoff Street.

There was no way of continuing the game of hide-and-seek, or of beating it. Tola'at Shani stopped short in front of me and said, "You wanted to talk to me," he gasped, "about my book."

"Yes," I answered. "I'm glad we met."

We had reached what in Westerns is called "the showdown," the part where the sheriff and the villain face each other in the middle of the deserted street for the final accounting, with muted strings in the background softly playing "Do not forsake me, Oh my darling!" Dizengoff Street, too, was suddenly devoid of acquaintances. As a matter of fact I can hardly remember ever having seen so few people on it.

We walked a few steps without saying anything. I tried to visualize the book, at least what it looked like, but all I could remember was the brown paper in which it was still wrapped. If at least I knew what was inside – a novel, short stories, a play, a collection of poems, essays?

We walked two blocks in a brown study. By the time we rounded the corner of Gordon Street, I had to say something.

"One thing is certain," I ventured. "You put a lot of work into that book!"

"Three years," Tola'at Shani whispered. "But I have carried the subject in me ever since before the war."

"One can feel that," I remarked. "It's a mature work."

We walked another few steps. Silence all around. No one disturbed us. Friends in need indeed!

"So what do you say?" Tola'at Shani asked in a weak voice.

"I'm impressed."

"By everything in it?"

I evaded the trap. Tola'at Shani was watching me out of the corner of his eye. Had I now answered, "Yes, by everything," he would have realized that I had not read his book and would have hated me for the rest of his life.

"I'll be quite frank with you," I therefore said. "The beginning is not so hot."

"You too?" Tola'at Shani sighed, resignedly. "You too, haven't got more sense? Isn't it crystal clear that the beginning is nothing more than an exposition?"

"Exposition, shmexposition," I shrugged. "What difference does it make? The question is, does the book grip you or doesn't it?"

Tola'at Shani became so sad that I felt sorry for him. But for Heaven's sake, why does he have to write such dull expositions?

"Later on you really get going," I consoled him. "Your characterization is very powerful. There is atmosphere, rhythm."

"Do you think I ought to have pruned the descriptive part by half?"

"If you had pruned out half the book would have been a winner."

"Maybe so," Tola'at Shani answered icily. "But don't you think I had to justify what made Boris join the rebels?"

Boris!

"Yes, Boris is certainly a character I won't forget so soon," I had to admit. "It's obvious you like him a great deal."

Tola'at Shani stared at me, panic-stricken.

"I like Boris? That swine? I think he's the most despicable type I ever created."

"Maybe that's what you think," I scoffed. "I'm telling you that in your innermost self you identify yourself with him!"

Tola'at Shani went pale.

"That really kills me," he broke down, and added, "As I started writing I really hated Boris, but when he becomes involved in that quarrel with Peter and the Naval Attaché and yet does not tell his mother about Avigail's rape – remember?"

"Do I remember? When he doesn't tell her –"

"That's right. So I asked myself: isn't Boris, in spite of his aberrations and fickle-mindedness, more of a man than the zoologist?"

"We are all human," I remarked tolerantly. "Some are like this, others like that, but in essence all are equal."

"Exactly!"

Had I read the book after all? Subconsciously, unconsciously, without noticing?

"They say," Tola'at Shani remarked haltingly, "that this is my strongest book plotwise."

I sent up a searching glance at a second-floor window, as if I were mentally reviewing his intellectual output. I have not yet read a thing by him. As a matter of fact, who is this Tola'at Shani? Why the hell does he keep sending me his books?

"I wouldn't say it's the best book you ever wrote" – I always put things in perspective – "but it certainly is one of the most suspenseful."

Tola'at Shani stopped dead in his tracks and I could see that I had touched a raw spot. So what? Do I have to fall flat on my face every time his pen touches paper? By the way, any chance to escape had now vanished. We did not meet anyone, although we had circled Dizengoff Circus twice.

"I knew it, I knew it, so help me." The bitterness welled up from the writer's throat, wounded as he was by my critical stance. "You mean the dinner in the apartment of the Storm Troop commander, don't you? I could have sworn that your chauvinism would balk at that! But what did you expect me to do, give everything that happened in the flooded valley a thick coating of saccharine? If you remember the – the –"

"Don't stutter," I admonished him. "There's a limit to my patience."

"Excuse me," Tola'at Shani continued obstinately. "When I gave a detailed description of the nocturnal camel race around the sheikh's harem, you liked it, didn't you?"

"You bet I did," I consented. "That was quite jolly."

"And when Ecaterina broke the lamp on the judge's desk, that you accepted, didn't you?"

"Well, that's reasonable."

"Then pardon me, but you also have to admit the debunking of Meir Kronstadt and his likes!"

"Ho-ho, my boy." I revolted inwardly. "For all I care you may slander the whole world, but you had better leave Meir Kronstadt alone!" I began to dislike the turn the conversation had taken. In a moment the sparks would start flying. I also discovered the reason for our splendid isolation. All the acquaintances we saw approaching in the distance suddenly disappeared as if the earth had swallowed them. Only I am abandoned here, damn it! The chauvinist in me raised his ugly head.

"Listen, Tola'at Shani," I said. "I wouldn't be so proud of that Kronstadt if I were you!"

"I am proud!"

The blood rushed to my head. He dares to contradict me!

"Kronstadt is a phony and therefore completely unconvincing," I declared. "You could drop him entirely without the book suffering in the least!"

"You are joking," Tola'at Shani spluttered. "And how are you going to build up the central conflict, may I ask?"

"Well, how?"

"You must be thinking of the zoologist!"

"Who else?"

"And Ecaterina?!"

"Let her go with the judge."

"In her ninth month?"

"After the confinement."

"Wise guy. Did you forget she gets run over?"

"So don't get her run over! Why must she get run over? Let Avigail get run over!"

"Excuse me, but that's ridiculous!"

That made me lose my temper completely. I have practically

never stopped reading for the past thirty years or so and I don't want to hear such childish remarks, O.K ?

"So you think it's ridiculous, my boy" – I turned on the decibels – "and your stupid camel race, what do you think that is? Frankly, I felt nauseated."

"That was precisely my aim! That you should feel nauseated! That you should see yourselves the way you really are!"

We had switched over to personal insults. Tola'at Shani was yellow with anger; his breath came in gasps.

"I know what's eating you!" He almost choked. "That I dared avoid banal solutions, right? That Boris did not drown under the cofferdam!"

Boris! He was all I needed right now!

"Leave me alone with your Boris!" I jeered at Tola'at Shani. "You are literally in love with that crook! If you must know it, his affair with Avigail is not at all relevant!"

"Not relevant?" the promising author groaned. "But she has to attach herself to someone, hasn't she?"

"All right, let her! But why to Boris? Is there no one else?"

"Who?" Tola'at Shani screamed and, grabbing me by the lapels, began to shake me. "*Who?*"

"That zoologist for instance – what's his name? – Kronstadt!"

"He isn't a zoologist!"

"He *is* a zoologist, and if not Kronstadt, then the commander of the Storm Troop!"

"Kronstadt *is* the commander of the Storm Troop!"

"There you are! For all I care, he may be even a meteorologist, anyone but Boris! Even the Naval Attaché is more logical! Or Peter! Or Birnbaum!"

"Who is Birnbaum?"

"Another male! No worse than Kronstadt, I can assure you! Scrawlings on patient paper do not yet make a book! You also need a plot, old boy, and heroes, and some inner conflict! Depth!"

By then it was I who was strangling him.

"*Depth*," I roared, "not blah-blah, no graphomaniacal outpourings, not abracadabra! Boris! What next? You call this a book? It's trash, my boy, rubbish! It won't go down with the public, take my word. I've got a nose for these things. No one will read your book! I didn't read it either!"

"You didn't read it?"

"*No!* Nor am I going to!"

I turned my back on him. For all I know he's still standing, dumbfounded, in the middle of Dizengoff Circus. The ass.

THE GREAT LITERARY FREAK SHOW

———————☐———————

The publisher took the manuscript out of his drawer and said to Tola'at Shani: "I've read them."

The poet slid to the edge of his chair. "Yes?" he whispered. "Yes?"

"Wonderful poems. I don't think anything as exquisite as *I Loved You, I Loved You* has been written in the last two hundred and fifty years."

"Thank you," Tola'at Shani breathed. "Thank you, Mr. Blau."

"Your collection of poems deserves a niche in world literature, I say. Bravo!"

"Thank you. I shall try to polish the poems to perfection before you publish them."

"Publish what?"

"Publish ... the book ... Mr. Blau. *I Loved You, I Loved You.*"

"Look here, I never said I was going to publish your poems."

"But ... you said ... wonderful...."

"Yes, they are very nice. But who buys poems nowadays?"

"I'm ready to renounce my writer's fee, Mr. Blau."

"That goes without saying. But it's not nearly enough."

"I'll make a small contribution toward costs."

"A fat lot of good that would do me. Perhaps you suffer from some fatal disease, T.S?"

"Why?"

"If I could put the book in a mourning jacket – 'the poet's last work' – that would push sales."

"I'm awfully sorry, but I'm healthy. At least for the time being. Maybe when the rains set in. . . ."

"I can't depend on miracles."

"So what can I do?"

"Now, I don't want to force your hand, but after the painter Zungspitz lost his eyesight, people paid fantastic prices for his canvases."

"Well, I wear glasses. . . ."

"T.S. You apparently have not yet grasped the principle of this thing. No work of art sells nowadays without hullabaloo and scandal."

"Say, Mr. Blau, I have an idea! I'll walk up and down Allenby Road stark naked with *I Loved You, I Loved You* under my arm."

"A hoary old trick. The sculptress Gizella Glick-Galgal has already stripped twice on Dizengoff Circus with an eye on her forthcoming exhibition. They say she will sell all her statues. You've got to get up early to get somewhere, my boy. Can you play the trumpet?"

"Not yet."

"That's a pity. So the only thing we can do is get violent. After the first unfavorable review you'll kick in the teeth of the reviewer. O.K?"

"Anything you say, Mr. Blau. But I'm afraid they'll only praise my poems."

"Oh, hell! Try to think. Perhaps you have some disease after all?"

"I'm desolate, but as I said. . . ."

"Or perhaps there was some insanity in your family? That should be a great help. When Joseph Melamed went out of his mind and was locked up, they sold three editions of his novel."

"Lucky devil!"

"That wasn't just luck. He realized that to push sales you need publicity. Are there any love poems in the collection?"

"Don't you remember, Mr. Blau?"

"I have not read your poems yet. But if there are daring, realistic descriptions, something could be done."

"No, Mr. Blau! I'd rather jump from a rooftop."

"That's an idea! 'Disappointed in his love, poet commits suicide.' Not bad at all. You could dedicate a poem to Meryl Streep."

"Why not? Who is she?"

"Never mind. All you have to do is write on the flyleaf: 'To my eternal love, M.S.'"

"All right."

"You know, I begin to like your book, T.S! We'll leak it to the press that you did two years for bigamy."

"That won't do. It happens to be true."

"Too bad. Is there anything anti-religious in your poems? Some offensive comment on Moses' character? The religious are very touchy on such matters. . . ."

"I don't remember. But I could add it."

"Splendid. If we can get the Rabbinate to ban your book, two editions of it are as good as sold."

"Thanks, Mr. Blau, thanks."

"Don't thank me yet! That's not all! Tonight you'll get yourself arrested for gate-crashing, smash a few windows, blow a trumpet in the men's room of the Dan Hotel, undress and catch TB."

"I'll try."

"Curse the Government, get converted and leave the country."

"All right."

"Don't come back, T.S., before you are a complete lunatic."

"That should be easy, Mr. Blau."

FLAPDOODLE

———————□———————

First the good news: after months of indecision, Zalman Shechter-mann & Co. finally resolved to publish Reuven Bar-On's novel *The Sellout*. Mr. Shechtermann himself invited the young author to his office.

"We'll print 350 copies to start with," he announced solemnly, "and then we'll see."

The young novelist was too excited to speak, and Shechtermann placed a fatherly arm around his shoulders and personally showed him to the door.

"I know, my boy, I know – 350 is a bit scrimpy, but people don't read as much as they used to. In fact, they don't read at all."

"What do you mean don't read?" said Bar-On. "We're the People of the Book!"

"So we are," the publisher agreed, "and the average Israeli is very proud of his books. Very careful of them, he is; keeps them in a neat row on his shelf and never touches them. Or if he does it's to glance at the last page. Or look for the juicy bits. Mostly, though, he only reads the flap. So go home, my boy, and write me a nice flap for your book."

"Me?" said the young writer uneasily. "You mean I myself . . . ?"

"Who else?" said Shechtermann. "No one knows more about you and your novel, right? Anyhow, who do you think writes those panegyrics on bookflaps if not the authors?"

"And the authors don't mind doing it? I mean, well . . . ."

"Na, nobody knows it, so what does it matter? Besides, they have no choice. Me, as the publisher, I certainly can't write it, because for that I'd have to read the book, and then I'd be prejudiced, see? Listen, if an author can't write his own flap, who can? Wait, let me show you."

Shechtermann went over to his desk and picked up a page of neatly typed flap copy.

"Here's what Finkelstein has given me for his latest: 'Israel's most popular storyteller, whose previous collection took the country by storm, offers his vast public a veritable feast of prose.' That's the sort of thing I want, see? Now go home, my boy, and lay it on with a trowel. No false modesty, eh?"

Bar-On went home, planted himself before his bookcase and read some dozen flaps for inspiration. Then he sat down and with blushing cheek wrote the first line about himself: "His haunting prose, his keen insight and his profound grasp of human motivation make Reuven Bar-On one of the most outstanding young writers of our day."

Whereupon he went and looked at himself in the mirror and spat in his face and tore up what he had written and dropped the scraps into the trash can and went to bed greatly relieved.

"No," he whispered into his pillow, "no literary prostitution for me."

Next morning Bar-On woke up and heard an inner voice telling him that, after all, it was the oldest profession on earth. So he went to the kitchen and fished the compliments out of the trash can and stuck them together with adhesive tape. Then he read over what he had written and decided he hadn't really exaggerated that much, although perhaps he'd better add a few adverbs.

"His stunningly haunting prose," the new version began, "his piercingly keen insight, and the veritable magic of his grasp . . . ."

Flushed with creative joy, Bar-On was beginning to feel that here, for the first time in his life, he was reading the bare, unvarnished truth about himself.

Toward noon he flew into a sudden rage. "What do you mean *one* of the most outstanding young writers?" he scolded himself. "You are *the* youngest and *the* most outstanding writer of the whole bloody lot!"

The reaction soon set in, however. A great wave of shame and disgust swept over Bar-On, and he picked up the flap-to-be between thumb and forefinger, dropped it into the toilet, flushed it down and felt greatly relieved.

That evening passers-by saw a young man prowling the streets and muttering to himself: "A literary giant ... like a comet ... a meteor. . . ."

"Poor fellow!" said the passers-by. "He's got to write a flap for his book."

Next morning Bar-On tore up every single draft he had written and threw the scraps out of the window with a sigh of relief. Then he went out for a little stroll in front of his house, collected the stuff from the pavement and went home and burst into tears and rang up Shechtermann.

"Shechtermann," he groaned into the mouthpiece, "I can't do it. I'm dying of shame."

"That's all right," said the publisher crisply, "dead authors sell better. Besides, I've just had a piece of bad news: *Hawaii 5-0* is coming back on television. Frankly, I doubt if this is the best time to publish. . . ."

Young Bar-On rang off, snatched the flap MS. and made for the publisher's with such haste that he dropped three superlatives on the way. He flung the page contemptuously at Shechtermann and stood there hating himself while Shechtermann cast his eye over it. "Hm, not bad," said the publisher at last. "Needs just a tiny bit of cutting. See? I told you only the writer himself could give an authentic picture."

Shechtermann picked up a pencil, changed a few words, cut a phrase here, added one there, and gave a satisfied nod over his final version, which read: "Zalman Shechtermann & Co., the publishing house of quality, brings you the best of Hebrew literature in convenient, inexpensive form. Zalman Shechtermann & Co. is proud to offer this unexpurgated novel, beautifully printed and bound, at the reduced price of only Sh.79·95. Soon to be published in this series is the top American bestseller *The Bordello: A Historical Survey.* Lavishly illustrated. Order your copy now!"

Bar-On came and read it over the publisher's shoulder.

"This?" he asked hoarsely, "This is the flap?"

"Yes," said Shechtermann. "Why?"

"But you said the author himself always wrote it."

"Oh, well," said Shechtermann, "if you insist." And he picked up his pencil again and wrote "Author's Statement" under the text.

Reuven Bar-On slunk out of the office, went home and proceeded to hang himself. Presently he felt the rope gettting rather tight about his neck and, afraid it would strangle him, he cut it and felt greatly relieved.

NOBLESSE OBLIGE

———□———

That morning at 4 A.M. the Swedish Foreign Minister received an urgent summons to the Libyan Ambassador. The stunned Minister was hush-rushed through the deserted streets of Stockholm at dawn, and ushered unceremoniously into the Libyan diplomat's bedroom.

"Telegram from Tripoli," his pyjamaed excellency informed him. "The President of the Republic, Colonel Gaddafi, wishes to receive this year's Nobel Prize for Literature."

"For literature?"

"Yep. Literature. Fiction."

"I'm awfully sorry, Your Excellency," said the Minister, "but the Swedish Academy is an independent body and its members are absolutely neutral."

"Fine," said the Ambassador, "so neutralize them."

"I mean, Your Excellency, that there is no way of influencing their decision."

"Right," hinted the Libyan diplomat, "so no more oil."

He demanded a written undertaking by noon. The Swedish Cabinet went into emergency session, as Arab oil makes up 61 per cent of the consumption of their unhappy industrial country. The Cabinet sat for 22 hours non-stop, then announced that it had discussed "problems of a cultural exchange with Libya."

Colonel Gaddafi interpreted this as a slap in the face and had a nervous fit in the tent set up for him inside the royal clinic. The youthful president tore off his clothes and flung them out of the window: "Churchill got the Nobel Prize for Literature twice," he shrieked, "just because he was white!"

In view of the Colonel's deep religious convictions, all the muezzins in his country declared a total embargo on "Zionist Sweden." Anyhow, the flow of oil to the giant tankers in the harbors of Libya was cut off at once. The Swedish Premier asked for an urgent audience with the Ambassador to stress the traditional friendship between their two peoples.

"Colonel Gaddafi is certainly entitled to put up his candidacy for the Nobel Prize," the Premier pointed out, "but framing it as an ultimatum isn't quite done." As an interim solution he offered to rebuke Israel in particularly harsh terms for its sluggishness in solving the Palestinian problem, but by then the microphones were already broadcasting President Gaddafi's great speech in Bengazi's main square: "That commie Solzhenitsyn *can* get the Nobel Prize for Literature," the leader roared, "the Jew Agnon can *too*, but an Arab nationalist *can't!*"

Gaddafi thereupon resigned and swore he'd retreat to the desert and grow carobs. The weeping mob burnt the American library out of sheer habit, yelling in chorus: "No-bel! Ga-dda-fi! No-bel! Ga-dda-fi!"

An official delegation of furious demonstrators set out to march on Oslo. Things grew hot in Libya and cold in Sweden, where severe restrictions were imposed on the use of transport, electricity and water closets. A stormy student demonstration clamored for an immediate severance of relations with "those loony tyrants in Tel Aviv."

Pressured by public opinion, the Academy went into another extraordinary session and discussed the world literary crisis *in camera*. It was leaked that the Academy has established beyond doubt that the Colonel could read and write perfectly well, even if his reading was confined to the Koran, in large print.

In view of these novel revelations, the Scandinavian press suggested a more realistic prize policy. The Swedish Premier flew to Tripoli. Rumor said he had offered Gaddafi the Nobel Prize for Chemistry in recognition of his achievements in the petrochemical field. The Libyan President flew into a rage and declared he'd never been so insulted in his life. He assured the stricken Premier that his revenge would be horrible indeed, and kicked him out of his tent.

By the time the Premier was on his flight back to Sweden, Oslo was already in flames, since the Libyan marchers had set fire to the Norwegian capital by mistake. Within a week two Italian passenger planes were blown up at Bombay airport by a new terror movement called "Palestinian Youth for Literary Justice," secretly trained and financed by nobody-knows-who.

The heating was switched off in every Swedish home and the population started piling up the furniture for bonfires. The Libyan Ambassador called in the King and wagged a finger at him: "C'mon, Gusti, what're you waiting for?"

From somewhere in Arabia, Uganda's ex-premier Idi Amin sent a 14,850-word cable to the Swedish Government demanding that they order Nobel to give all his prizes to Gaddafi right away or else, indicating that troops still loyal to him would go to Stockholm and smash it to bits. The Swedish Government rejected his threats in a stiff diplomatic note to Riyadh.

The ruling Social-Democratic Party warned against any hasty military steps, and its official organ published an editorial analyzing the importance of the cultural revolution initiated by "this youthful Colonel brimming with vigor and energy." They praised his brilliant speeches for their "religio-mystical appeal" and himself for "infusing militant Islam with a noble spirit."

President Mitterand offered to mediate, and suggested dividing the prize between France's most brilliant computer poet and Gaddafi, but the Colonel just smiled bitterly and stopped the oil supply to France for two days.

Then came the snow and the Swedish merger proposal to Libya: one constitution, one army, joint foreign policy and psychiatric institutions. Gaddafi's reply: Literature or Nothing! By now there were no more candles to be had in Sweden for love or money.

At this stage the Academy published its advance decision on the 1989 Nobel Prize for Literature. Next day the oil started flowing into the tankers again.

□ *The following stories are a merry obituary to a living institution – the theater.*

It is safe to assume that the theater is one of mankind's oldest institutions: the expulsion from Paradise had all the makings of a theatrical performance, played with remarkable amateurishness by the couple and with quite unnecessary pathos by the seraph with his flaming sword. The Serpent was most convincing, especially in the pantomime parts, but it is a well-known fact that the villain always steals the show. The critics panned the extravaganza mercilessly. Ever since, man has been touring the world, putting on terrible shows.

The real difficulty started when it was found that man needed an audience. In some underground cave, by the flickering light of a glob of burning fat, a big ape for the first time clapped his two paws together, and thus invented applause. That set off a chain reaction, Man decided to build himself a stage enclosed on three sides, and to write his lines beforehand but make believe that this was not so. His enthusiasm even carried over to his audience, which began to play out a part itself, the part of a person taking this absurd behavior at face value. What is more, despoilers of widows and oppressors of orphans for thousands of years shed genuine tears whenever someone on the stage despoiled widows or oppressed orphans. Even the widows and the orphans liked it: "Just like life," they'd say, "just like life!" It was an excellent take-off.

THE NIGHT OF THE LONG KNIVES

―――――□―――――

The official opening of *Unfair to Goliath* was over by 9:30 P.M. The show took fifteen minutes less than planned because the critics did not applaud, only the claque of relatives and friends. We too, the spiritual parent of *Goliath*, clapped surreptitiously, but the group of reviewers got up at once and left in a gaggle. They were headed by Clive Barnes of the *New York Times*, struggling into his winter coat. Joe, our producer, claims that he saw him smile once in the first act, but Dick, the director, thinks that he was just picking his teeth. In any case, Barnes left much too fast. A cold wind blew down the aisles. Jerry Tallmer, the prestigious reviewer of the *New York Post*, had left twenty minutes before the end, his face livid with rage.

As he passed us in the aisle Dick had a seizure. "He's leaving," he groaned. "He's leaving, he's leaving."

I was beyond caring. During the intermission, when we hadn't dared move out of our seats lest we provoke the gods' ire, I had made up my mind to take the first plane back home and ask the government for asylum. It is said the airlines always reserve a few seats for refugees from Broadway first nights. I have a severe case of butterflies and can't catch any of them. Joe is the calmest, only he can't close his left eye and it blinks in the darkness like a phosphorescent button.

"Well," he keeps asking Bernstein, our PR man, "what do you think?"

"We'll see."

We hug the actors, not unlike early Christians stepping into the arena. We have only three-quarters of an hour left to love each other. the first TV reviews will then arrive and we will sink into limbo filled with primeval hatred. We all know the fateful ratio: out of ten New York shows, eight close down on the day following the première, one

44

agonizes for a few weeks, and one . . . maybe. . . .

Jerry Tallmer had left before the end.

The time is 11:00. We sit in Bernstein's office, in front of the TV set without speaking a word. Present: Joe and his wife, Dick, myself, Menahem (the young Israeli composer) and the seven actors. The announcer prattles some nonsense about Nixon and Vietnam and other quite marginal things. I am slightly bothered by the rushing noise in my ears; my heart throbs like a jungle drum. Actually, I am here only in the technical sense, for my tortured soul has long since been playing at home with Amir and Ranana. From time to time I mumble a prayer, that's all.

11:15. We stop breathing. Dick lies motionless; his hair starts graying at the temples. Only Bernstein puffs contentedly on his cigar (he is an *habitué* at funerals). In his hands he holds a small tape recorder to record the station announcer for quotable quotes. At long last he appears: Stuart Klein of CBS.

"Sharp . . . self-mocking humor . . . pointed fun."

Joe jumps up from his chair and lets go with a succession of guttural yells. We all clap our hands. This is how the Jews must have felt when Moses struck the rock and water gushed forth. However, Moses had better odds. Out of ten strikes, at least three were bound to succeed. We embrace, hop around the room and I send Amir and Ranana packing. Menahem levitates. Klein spoke well of us, Klein loves us, Klein is great.

"A hit!" Joe yells. "We have got a hit! A hit!" He embraces me warmly and whispers in my ear. "I knew why I brought you over from Israel. I knew what I was doing."

I love him myself, because he is a good man. His wife proposed that I settle down in New York and that together we open a department store. But for the fact that the actors are gentiles, we would by now be doing the *hora*. I can see in their eyes that they are seriously considering conversion. If NBC praises us as well, nothing will stop them from running to the nearest rabbi.

11:20. Edwin Newman, the granddad of all panners, appears on the screen. Burning eyes are glued to his ill-boding pate. We are thirsty for praise, sir, lots of praise, with lots and lots of adjectives.

"Quiet!" Bernstein roars. "I am recording!"

Newman works according to the Chinese-torture method. He wastes most of the minute he is on the air on philosophical thoughts, on the meaning of humor and its purpose in the civilization of mankind. He is simply killing us. He knows only too well that we are sitting hypnotized around the set, so he drags out the passing of sentence. One frown from him and we close down tomorrow. As he comes to the end, we are more dead than alive.

"Altogether," Newman pontificates with sadistic relish, "it was a pleasant evening."

Joe collapses. Dick rushes out to fetch some water and fails to return. The actors fan their faces. We survived TV and are still alive. Now it is the turn of the three large dailies: the *Times*, the *Post* and the *Daily News*. Should even one be con, we close. (We don't mention it, but Jerry Tallmer did leave early.) Silence. Bernstein is trying to establish contact with spies planted in the newspaper offices. The *Daily News* is the first to respond. A nervous and muffled voice quickly reads into the receiver the marvelous – repeat marvelous – review of Mr. Silver, may he go from strength to strength. We are good-natured, witty, perceptive, fantastic.

Joe clasps me in his strong arms. "Genius," he breathes in my ear. "You're a once-in-a-century genius."

I believe him; he is the expert. The producer has a quick powwow with his friends. They intend adopting me as their son. Why not? We could talk it over. Dick takes a piece of paper and, in a shaking hand, figures out how much the swimming pool would cost in the villa he is going to build soon. Joe buys up the Empire State Building, a fleet of tankers, and even pays back some of his debts. I transfer my gains into the custody of the collector of Internal Revenue within the framework of a package deal which leaves me with mixed feelings.

12:15. The telephone rings. The *Times* spy reports. He has got the first two columns, filched at danger to his life, from the proofreader's desk. We are recording; the pulse beat is 103. This is Clive Barnes, folks, the Pope; he by himself outweighs sixty other reviewers.

"This is a nice little show, pleasant and heart-warming. . . ."

These were the happiest three seconds in our whole lives. A miracle, that was the general feeling; an almost incredible Biblical miracle was taking place before our eyes. The Lord has chosen us to rule over the nations. There must be something in us which disarms critics, radioactive, anti-panning bodies. My associates are building air-conditioned castles in Spain, complete with swimming pools. Only the experienced Bernstein is grim-faced. He didn't like the word "little." He knows why.

And then something terrible happens.

"But," the intelligence agent mumbles into the receiver at the end of those three happy seconds, "this show lacks panache and is too long."

"Lacks . . . panache . . . too long. . . ."

My heart stops beating. Joe goes white and grips his head. These four words have brought down our victory arch around our heads. True, Barnes added about a dozen compliments on my great humanity and things like that, but this is no longer the Song of Songs; this is simply an excellent review and that is not enough for survival on Broadway. Menahem utters strange sighs, Joe's wife bursts into tears, Dick's white hair starts falling out. And these are just the first two columns of the *Times*, and Jerry Tallmer left before the. . . .

"What shall we do?" Joe asks his court P R man, and his voice sounds as if it comes from the grave. "Do we close?"

Bernstein stares into the air. He rolls the fateful words on his tongue and tastes them for effect: lacks panache . . . too long. . . .

"We could save a few good quotes from his review for the ads," he decides in the end. "For twenty grand it could carry on a few weeks."

He means $20,000.

The actors get up quietly and leave the room without saying another word. They are contacting their agents right away for new jobs. I feel terribly lonely. Amir and Ranana are back in my arms. Dick goes on suffering in a corner.

Joe stares at me out of his wide-open left eye. "They warned me," he barks. "They warned me against Israeli directors."

His wife motions to me to beat it before they lose their tempers. I go to pieces, turn into salvage. Menahem whispers to me in Hebrew, "The main thing is health." Stupid *sabra*.[1] I hate Menahem with a burning passion. I hate Dick as well. He also hates me. And Bernstein. The P R man records the end of the *Times* phone call. Dick leaves the room; he doesn't want to hear.

"Excellent performances," the reviewer surprises us. "A very talented cast, very pleasant atmosphere."

Things start looking up. Joe collects his limbs scattered all over the room and gets up. His wife comes over to me and strokes my hair. The time is 1:30. May the Lord have pity on us. It all depends on Barnes's ending.

"I enjoyed a lot of it," the great Barnes ends.

"No!" Joe jumps up, shouting hoarsely, and drives his fist against the wall. "No!"

"What happened?"

"If he had said, 'I enjoyed it a lot,' we would have been a smash hit right away!"

Bernstein also opines that this little difference in wording could well cost us a million dollars.

We sprawl out, spent, on the carpet when a special-service delivery man brings us – for an exorbitant fee – the proofs from the *Post*. Nobody dares read them. Before us again appears the receding figure of Jerry Tallmer.

Bernstein lifts the proofs with a limp hand and looks at the review with knitted brows.

Eerie silence.

"Well," a voice out of the grave asks, "what does he say?"

---

[1] A *sabra* is a native-born Israeli.

"This," Bernstein says, "is simply a rave review."

Fireflies dance in front of our eyes, and I distinctly hear the chorus from Beethoven's Ninth. What a man, what a reviewer, this Jerry Tallmer! Others, those pygmies, have to sit till the end of a show, but an intellectual of his caliber knows at once what is good and what is bad. Of course he left before the end. That's only natural. What a man!

"My nose never fools me," Joe whispers. "I knew you would pull it off."

Menahem does not move; he must have died or something. We'll have to see about another pianist. As a matter of fact, no one is moving in the room. The kudos of the wire agencies and the roundup of the radio stations will find only our dead bodies. Joe slowly puts a hand in his pocket, pulls out the checkbook and writes out $6,000 for next day's victory ads. But deep inside he is crying. If Clive Barnes had written "it a lot" instead of "a lot of it" he would be practically a millionaire. Anyway the show goes on. My feet drag me outside into the dawn light. In the lobby I glance in the mirror and get a shock at the sight of the crazed gentleman staring back at me from eyes sunk deep in their sockets. Maybe little Goliath has won, but his daddy will never be the same again.

□ As Topol learned from his own experience in London, it is a beautiful Jewish tradition to invite a few hungry beggars to our loaded tables. This beautiful tradition is being kept going in our modern state as well, with the minor modification that as a rule, nowadays, the beggar is expected to pick up the tab.

THE NIGHT OUR HAIR
TURNED GRAY

———————□———————

The premiere was over and we duly stepped backstage and congratulated the architects of victory, then assembled in front of the theater to talk things over in earnest. The mood was jubilant, because the show was obviously a bomb.

Then Kunstatter asked, I clearly remember him asking, "Say, how about a bite?"

We reacted with uninhibited glee. Somebody mentioned the new Balalaika restaurant with its cultivated French cuisine. Though we realized that prices would be rather high at such a chic eatery, the show had been so enjoyably lousy that we decided this was no time for penny-pinching.

It was quite a place – the walls covered with red rugs, intimate candlelight, the ceiling of wood and the waiters from the south of France. They pulled up six tables for us, and only then did we notice that no less than twenty people had come along, among them a number of complete strangers. This is almost unavoidable – people on the fringe of show business always follow celebrities wherever they go.

We ordered the appetizer and the main dish, although the price list confirmed our worst fears. But the food was glorious, the wine heady, the conversation sparkling, so what the hell?

I had just finished the oven-baked chops when the little one gently poked me in the ribs.

"Ephraim," she whispered, "look!"

My glance swept the length of the table. Strange, I mused, several chairs had become vacant. Those who had sat in them had apparently finished their meal and vanished. Altogether, twelve were left, including ourselves. "They fall who go first," the old military adage says, but there is no intimation anywhere that they have to pay before going.

I looked around searchingly. The headwaiter in his gleaming tuxedo was standing in a strategic corner, raising his bushy eyebrows, taking notes.

I returned my gaze to my fellow diners: there was a certain look of dejection about them. A hidden fear was flickering in their eyes, a fear which cannot be fully expressed in words, but if pressed would translate as: "Who's going to pay for this?"

The next head count showed only ten celebrants left. Another couple had left under the cloak of the intimate lighting. Conversation dragged, unbearable tension took over. No one dared look his fellow in the eye, gears were audibly grating as we computed the exorbitant prices.

Gradually, glances focused on Kunstatter.

From a strictly moral point of view, it was only fair that he should pay. After all, it had been his invitation, his stupid idea to have a bite. What had been his exact words? Let's see: "Come on, friends," he had said, "come and have dinner with me," or perhaps he had even said, "Be my guests tonight, folks," or words to that effect. Without a doubt he was our man. He was also honest. He would pay.

All eyes were on Kunstatter.

Kunstatter finished his meal with disconcerting calm and ordered coffee. We held our breath, our nostrils flared. If Konstatter now turned to us and asked "Coffee, anyone?" that would establish his responsibility, his host status and his willingness to bear the consequences. But Kunstatter sipped his coffee with a noncommittal face and talked to his wife.

Meanwhile a few more rats had fled the sinking ship. The passenger list had shrunk to seven lost souls.

Who's going to pay?

The lively conversation had long ago fizzled out. Now and then we exchanged a few grunts about Afghanistan and the latest divorces in town, but this was just a pretext for passing to the "everybody fend for himself" stage. Now every additional desertion would increase the danger of having to pay. It was obvious that all those left were alert to the danger.

Then a terrible thing happened.

One of the hostages, Ben-Zion Ziegler, rose with demonstrative nonchalance and said: "Excuse me, I must call the office."

And with measured steps he escaped from our field of vision. Cold sweat ran down our brows. Only then did we realize that he had come alone, without his wife, thereby enjoying superior mobility.

Ben-Zion Ziegler never returned.

Weeks later, eyewitnesses related that he had indeed entered a phone booth and, upon leaving it, had languidly waved toward us and passed through the main entrance. No one had seen him waving. When did he wave? And what if he had waved?

Who's going to pay?

More dropouts increased the tension. Personally, I cursed the recklessness which had made the little one and myself sit with our backs to the waiters, unable to see what they were plotting in the background. This weakened my position to the point of making it eminently dangerous. Any moment now, the headwaiter would show up at our backs . . . the check under a napkin on the plate . . . and I would have no room for maneuver. Terrible!

"Excuse me." Kunstatter suddenly jumped to his feet, consulting his watch with great concern. "The babysitter . . . !"

And before we could gather our wits he left with his wife. Engineer Glick rose as if intending to shout something after him, but not a word left his gasping throat. Unmitigated panic broke out.

Kunstatter had been our last hope. After his desertion only three hapless couples were left: the Glicks, the Bar Honigs and us.

I looked behind me. The waiter was standing in his corner, never letting us out of his sight. Never in my life have I seen such bushy eyebrows.

How much would the check be? Twenty lamb chops ... Goodness!

Mrs. Bar Honig started jabbering Polish with her husband. Even without an interpreter, we all understood what the shouting was about. What's more, we answered categorically, albeit mutely:

"I'm not willing either, you witch!"

The main thing was not to give in! The little one, chalk-white, gripped my damp hand under the table. It's a good feeling to know that in life's critical moments one is not alone. That gave me the strength to concentrate on our plight. Because it was clear that from now on the battle was to the death. One careless step and you are finished. So, just don't lose your head, hold out, old boy! Whoever shows the first sign of wavering or inner weakness, whoever gives the slightest hint to the waiter – he'll pay the check.

Before the mind's eye there arose tragic cases in which innocent people had paid at the end of the meal for the whole gathering, just because they had lifted a hand to chase away a fly. In such cases the waiter swoops down straight on the signaler and discreetly hands him the check. No signals, no moves! The reader probably knows those horrible moments when several couples are sitting at the table and the waiter stands within range with his plate of numbers, his eyes roaming left and right in the oppressive silence. One ages years in such moments. If you just shake your head, move your hand ever so slightly toward your pocket, you've had it. You pay. These are elementary rules. So keep cool!

The time was 3:00 A.M. For the last two hours we had been all by ourselves in the restaurant, completely isolated from the outside world. But no one dared propose that we leave, because he who called the waiter would also have to pay the check.

But what's that?

Suddenly I felt my wife's hand turning ice-cold. In a flash I decoded her message. Bar Honig and Engineer Glick suddenly started talking with disgusting eagerness. They talked with alacrity and cut into each other's words. The blood drained from my head. I felt that the moment of truth had come. Somewhere in the recesses of the restaurant the waiter had started moving toward me. . . .

I had only a few seconds left. My brain worked feverishly. Clearly, they were isolating me in preparation for the debacle. The waiter would come, see that I was the only accessible man at the table, and naturally. . . .

I closed my eyes and decided to try a finesse.

There was no choice. Only by bluffing could I hope to save my skin. I would try to make the other two believe that I was willing and ready to settle the check, and thus gain their confidence, so that at the last moment, when my hand was already in my pocket, one of them would swallow the bait and, prompted by his European manners, would make a gesture and mumble: "Hey, let me do that." Whereupon I would immediately retreat – "Please!" – and leave him with the bill! This is called the Haifa Gambit because it is said to have been devised by a Haifa industrialist two years ago on New Year's Eve.

I therefore turned round and called out loudly: "Waiter! The check!"

Bar Honig and Glick stopped talking, pleasantly surprised, and dropped back, exhausted. I pulled out my wallet with a sweeping movement so as to dispel any doubt in their hearts and counted up to three: 1–2–3. But tonight Haifa failed dismally – no one swallowed the bait. They kept mum as a shoal of fish. Their noses quivered slightly and their eyes were downcast. That's all. Engineer Glick even managed a sadistic grin. I hated them.

I lifted the napkin with two fingers and peeped:

"*760 shekels.* . . ."

"Only sign, please," the waiter said. "Mr. Kunstatter put everything on his account before he left."

☐ *We are said to have a labor regime. That does not mean to say that the workers actually dominate the government. They simply have the upper hand in each separate plant and enterprise, even in the theaters.*

We are therefore the only country in the world where the humblest scenery shifter earns more than the greatest character actor. (According to our economists, this anomaly is dictated by the law of supply and demand, i.e. everybody wants to become a great actor, nobody an unskilled scene shifter.)

Our largest theaters function on a cooperative basis, with the actor and the electrician enjoying equal rights, except that the actor is not paid overtime, because one can never make enough sacrifices for art.

Occasionally our actors rise in revolt against the totalitarian rule of the working class, but the revolt generally ends on a note as hopeless as Hamlet's great soliloquy or the Tibetan revolt against Red China.

MUNDEK versus SHAKESPEARE

———☐———

I entered the café to phone my wife that I was coming, and immediately jumped back, but too late. Jarden Podmenitzki, the noted character actor, had spotted me and approached with wide-open arms.

"Take a seat," he said. "Have a drink."

Jarden Podmenitzki looked unusually careworn, although as far as I knew there was no première in the offing. He had black rings under his eyes and the skin was taut on his broad Slavic cheekbones.

"You don't look too well," I said. "I won't trouble you."

"Sit down and have a drink. If you promise not to write about it, I'll tell you what's eating me."

"Unfortunately I can't guarantee publication."

"Mundek."

"Beg your pardon?"

"Mundek. That man is killing me."

"Who is Mundek?"

"What? You don't know Mundek? Say, what's the matter with you? Mundek is the theater's oldest scene shifter. And if I kick the bucket one of these days, the world will have Mundek to blame for it."

"What do you think of Gorbachev's latest statement?"

"He's a mountain of a man, bursting with energy and completely toothless. I don't know how he came to be in the theater. He says he founded it. I don't want you to take me for a die-hard reactionary. Quite the contrary, I am a great friend of the working class, but this Mundek sometimes makes me long for the good old capitalistic system. Look: the country is lying at my feet, wherever I go I'm feted and toasted – you know this only too well – and yet this Mundek treats me as if I were some silly extra. Imagine: I was reciting my great monologue from Shakespeare's *Richard III* at the deathbed of my father whom I have just poisoned – 'Your soul's vagrant scream tears / Me Sire who were king / Among mortals and steel / Blade carved out what / Uttering a hundred deaths I'd die.' As I said, I was reciting my great monologue, with the public hanging on my lips, when suddenly, about two yards from me, just behind the western battlement, he rises, blows his nose, and says to the other stagehands, '*Kinder, efsher voln mir shpiln a bissele kurtn?*'*He says this in Yiddish, because that's the only language he speaks, and so loudly that it carries to the last row. Now I ask you, how could I throw myself on my father's body, steeped in grief and transcendental wisdom, when all the while I can see Mundek and his pals sitting on the executioners' axes, playing cards as if the world belonged to them? What would you do in my place?"

"I would tell them to stop it."

"Ach, sometimes you talk like a half-wit or a critic. You think they are reasonable? Mundek, for instance, brings with him every night half a pound of cheese, a loaf of bread, and two huge horseradishes. And about halfway through the second act, I have a love scene with the

*"Boys, how about a little game of cards?"

56

princess, whom I try to seduce. So every time I kneel down and hand her the gem-studded keys of the city, Mundek bites into his horse-radish, and by the noise you'd think you were at Lydda airport, to say nothing of the smell. I implored him, 'Mundek, for goodness' sake, try to have your dinner somewhat earlier or later, not just during my love scene, because I can't stand it.' Mundek said he could not help it, we'd have to move the scene, he was used to having his dinner at nine-thirty sharp. I said to him, 'So you think your horseradishes are more important than my love scene?' And he answered, 'That's right.' You know how he walks about backstage? Like an elephant. Or a mountain climber. A tank. The scenery shakes. Once I felt I couldn't stand it any longer. 'Don't stomp about during performances!' I bellowed. Mundek countered that he wasn't taking any orders from me. I lost my temper. 'You abject worm!' I roared. 'Who is the star here, you or I?' So Mundek asked me how much I was making. I said a hundred and forty-five before taxes, because I was ashamed of telling him the truth. 'You see,' Mundek said, 'I get three hundred and twenty-four without overtime.' He holds absolute power in his hands. When, for instance, Kirshberger is sick, he handles the curtain. Can you imagine how that works out? Perhaps you remember that at the end of the first act I turn toward my mother's ghost and say, 'Flames in the purple skies my heart's / Wells are drying up mother/ O passionate woman who gave / Me to the world your/ Husband's slayer is facing you' – in other words this is where I confess to having killed my father, the venerable Scottish laird. So what does Mundek do? Hardly do I say 'Flames in the purple skies my heart's when he starts lowering the curtain! Desperately I quicken my rendering, like a phonograph gone out of control, but at 'passionate woman' the curtain is down, and the public will forever wonder who killed my father. After the doctor revived me in the wings, I fell on Mundek, my hands still manacled. 'What's this?' I roared. 'What's this, you miserable twerp?' 'Shut up! Where do you think you are? This is a theater.' Mundek said, cutting me short. 'Believe me, it was high time I lowered that curtain. The play is too long, and we started rather late today. And besides, excuse me, but you were lousy and I couldn't stand your silly babble.' 'Man!' I screamed, 'this play is by Shakespeare!' 'I don't care if it's by Ben-Gurion,' Mundek retorted. 'I've been in the profession for thirty-seven years, and if Mundek tells you that you have to cut a play, you can bet your life he is right!'

"For a while I seriously considered committing suicide, but then I said to myself, 'No! I won't let this scoundrel drive me out of my mind.' You know what I did?"

"Bromide?"

"No. I burst without knocking into the manager's office. 'Look, Sulzberger,' I said. 'You know that I am not oversensitive, but one of these days your theater is going to lose Podmenitzki!' I told Sulzberger how every night, when the death knell fades out at the end of act three, and my victims' restless ghosts scurry across the stage in deathly silence, one can always hear a faint tinkling on the left: Mundek is spinning his car keys, signaling that it is late. And I also told Sulzberger that whenever I creep in the darkness toward the cross, dagger in hand, I always get a strong light from the right, because Mundek cannot light his cigarette anywhere else but behind the altar. 'Mundek,' I implored him, 'at least turn your back when you light that match.' 'A little light never hurt anybody,' Mundek answered, but that's still not everything. During the intermissions he always sits on my throne, and three times so far he has left his illustrated Yiddish paper on it. And after the third bell, he usually leaves his burning cigarette end on my crown. Several times smoke has come out of my head and everybody has laughed.

" 'I am the king,' I told him fiercely in the interval. 'I am the king, you jackal.' 'What king, who king?' that idiot jeered. 'You are Jarden Podmenitzki, a ham actor. A king doesn't play theater.' Can you imagine such a thing? For thirty-seven years he has been in the profession, and yet he doesn't realize what's happening onstage. I said to Sulzberger, 'Sulzberger, it's either me or Mundek!' He tried to calm me, saying that all these things would pass, Mundek would not live forever. But when I insisted and pressed too hard, he had to fire me. You understand? He fired Jarden Podmenitzki! Understand?"

"I understand," I said. "He fired you."

"Come now, you must realize what this means. I said to Sulzberger, 'So Mundek is more important than Podmenitzki?' And Sulzberger said, 'The hell he is, but I can't fire Mundek, because then all the stagehands will go on strike and there will be no show. Besides, according to trade union regulations, I'd have to pay Mundek thirty-five thousand shekels severance pay. Who dares touch these fellows?' In fact, Sulzberger is right. We actors will play whether we get our salaries or not. But try to make Mundek wait half a day for his overtime pay! I think Mundek must have got wind of my intervention with Sulzberger, because a terrible thing happened next day. You know, I have a big malediction scene at the beginning of the third act. I stand atop the fresh graves of my nephews and curse the Byzantines, and the light slowly fades, and as I stand there in my royal glory, my right hand raised in malediction, I disappear toward the left on the revolving stage. To cut a long story short, on that night the stage turned to the right. Naturally I fell on my face, and the scepter and orb rolled away, so that it was quite a job finding them in the darkness. After this, if I remember rightly, I had to undergo medical treatment for a couple of days, and even today, when I think of that evening, my limbs are seized with a queer trembling. It's all Mundek's doing. . . ."

"Look, Podmenitzki," I said comfortingly, "you are too big a giant to let the petty backbiting of such a nincompoop annoy you. Try not to think of this Mundek."

"If only I could! But what happened last night tops it all. Mundek, for the first time in his life, fell sick and didn't come to work. There was such quiet behind the scenes that it made me nervous. You know, I've become used to the coughing and tramping, to say nothing of the horseradish. Believe it or not, this is what I said at my father's death-bed: 'Your soul's vagrant scream tears / Me Sire who were king/ Among mortals and steel / Blade carved out *Kinder/ Efsher voln mir shpiln a bissele/ Kurtn* what uttering/ A hundred deaths I'd die.' Luckily, nobody in the audience noticed my slip, so gigantic is Shakespeare's genius. But I, Jarden Podmenitzki, am telling you that there is something infinitely tragic in Mundek's having become such an obsession with me."

O SOLO MIO

Our colleague, the late Mr. Shakespeare, whoever he may have been, was at least smart in one vital field: he took the main roles in his plays. In this way he saved himself a lot of trouble. On today's stage the actors rule supreme and every single one of them is a two-legged pressure group. We learnt about this fact of life in person when the manager of one of our more or less musical theaters approached us on the matter of a musical. We said to him: "Sir, I've never in my life written a musical, and besides I hate it when people break into song and dance without the slightest provocation."

Thereupon the manager replied: "Anyone can write a musical, my boy. The principle of it could not be simpler: in an opera one of the lovers always dies, while in a musical both are always saved. Try it, I am sure you will succeed! I won't meddle in your choice of subject, but it is most desirable that it should somehow include Puerto Rico because that place is very 'in' nowadays!"

At this point in our conversation, the director's assistant came in and handed over Mrs. Shinovski's latest message, to the effect that unless she, Felicia Shinovski, sings the solo part in the finale, she might as well drop out entirely from the musical, because that solo had been written especially for her.

I asked: "Excuse me, what finale is she speaking about?"

"Why, the finale of the musical you are going to write one of these days."

"But what is a 'solo'?"

"A 'solo' is a unique opportunity for the singer to earn applause onstage without any partners sharing the glory, while the other actors go green with envy and artistic frustration backstage."

After this brief course of instruction I went home and dashed off a very nice and topical libretto. That is, a young Israeli bookkeeper on a visit to Puerto Rico falls in love with a half-caste belly dancer, but her uncle, who is an honorary consul, will not agree to the marriage because according to tradition the girls in his family have to marry Norwegian princes, whereupon the bookkeeper pretends that he is indeed a Norwegian prince and it looks as if things are working out towards a happy end when suddenly the boy realizes that the dancer does not love him as a man but only as a bookkeeper because she had discovered that he is only a bookkeeper, although in fact he is not a bookkeeper but really a Norwegian prince, a king's bastard, while the dancer is a kibbutz member and the two take over the care of the poultry run. Curtain.

The manager listened spellbound to my story line which he found just perfect, except that he asked me to bring it more in line with the character of the musical, e.g. the boy should not be a bookkeeper but a rear admiral, because it was important that he should look good while singing his opening solo, and bookkeepers' uniforms are never as smart as rear admirals'.

"O.K." I said. "Let him be a rear admiral."

Just then there was a big commotion outside and the first tenor burst into the room and shouted that he had been eavesdropping behind the door and had heard that we wanted to make him a rear admiral, while every babe-in-arms knew that a rear admiral's solo always flopped. He wanted to be a full admiral, with no rear, and besides he was quitting, would they kindly strike him off the roster. . . . With that he dashed out. I trembled in every limb, but the manager kept remarkably cool and advised me to promote the tenor to the rank of admiral.

"What's the difference?" he said. "There is nothing to prevent an admiral from parachuting on Lod Airport."

"Why parachute? Why Lod?"

"Because one of my oldest actresses has a solo: 'Fly little bird, fly/ the sea is so dry/ fly and goodbye.' Without this solo she won't come to rehearsals."

"Oh, well. So the admiral spots a dancer in Lod. . . ."

"An air hostess."

"All right, an air hostess. . . ."

"Five air hostesses."

"Why five?"

"Because I have five prima donnas and none of them can be less of an air hostess than the other."

Here the assistant came in and informed the manager that Mrs. Shinovski was returning her "card solo" because she was not prepared to sing just three stanzas, but insisted on at least five.

The manager took the manuscript of the solo and informed Mrs. Shinovski that she was fired and could apply to the Labor Exchange. . . .

"Excuse me," I said, "what, as a matter of fact, is the 'card solo'?"

"Oh, I'm sorry, I forgot to tell you that in your musical, just before the finale, I am building a pagoda made up of bridge cards in natural colors and there Shinovski sings a solo in rumba rhythm."

"And . . . couldn't we . . . without those cards. . . ."

"No. The solo is ready. Its refrain is: 'Cards-boom-cards-boom . . . my cards-boom.' It's too late to change anything now."

The assistant came in and whispered in the manager's ear that Mrs. Shinovski had hanged herself on the rope of the fire curtain.

"Fine," the manager said, "so as I see it, the Second Act ends with the diplomat's visit to the Kurdistan Quarter."

"What diplomat?"

"The first tenor."

"But isn't he an admiral?"

"No. I need a political solo after all. Elections are just around the corner."

"O.K. But why the Kurdistan Quarter ?"

"I've got a Kurdistan Ballet number with two solo dancers. . . ."

The assistant came in and announced that Mrs. Shinovski wanted her solo back. The manager returned the manuscript, then turned to me and said: "Naturally, the Second Act opens with elephants."

"What elephants?"

"I rented eight elephants to introduce the solo of the comedian playing the Maharajah."

Here the comedian popped out from under the desk where he had been hiding for the past thirty-six hours, threw himself on the ground, and implored amidst contortions painful to witness: "No elephants . . . no elephants please. . . I'll fill up the stage all by myself . . . the elephants will only be in the way . . . it's either the elephants or me . . . sir."

"All right," the manager said, "get your check at the cashier's and beat it."

The comedian winced as if his face had been slapped, then drew up to his full height and left the room, walked over to the cashier's, collected his salary and stayed to study his solo.

"What now?" I asked the manager.

"Everything's under control," the manager assured me. "As it now stands, the play would run four and a half hours. We'll cut your story a bit, and then it should be just right."

The assistant came in and announced that the elephants were demanding a solo.

"Damn it," the manager erupted, "I can't give every elephant a solo!"

"You have to," the assistant retorted. "The elephants declared that otherwise they won't dance in the ballet. They claim that they are always being blocked from sight whenever they are onstage. . . ."

Suddenly the second tenor broke into pleasant song from behind the door: "O Solo Mio!" For the last fortnight he had been on a hunger strike demanding another solo as encore, otherwise he threatened he would go off his rocker and burn down the theater. The manager and myself climbed out of the window and slid down the drainpipe to avoid the juvenile lead who had been waiting to see the manager about a certain matter for the last two days and was now lying in ambush at the gate. I asked the manager how he could stand this madhouse. He looked at me greatly puzzled and assured me that as a matter of fact this had been a rather quiet, almost bucolic day.

EXIT

———□———

The cast of my musical – Tarzan of the Apes loses a fortune on cards and the elephants rescue it – the cast of my musical is no exception in its desire for exclusive solos. In the artistic consciousness of every great actor the stage is sublimated as a metaphysical, pseudo-natural-istic arena in which success is atavistically based on two solid elements: to stand alone on the boards and to talk a lot. Unfortunately, in most cases it doesn't work out that way. Playwrights prefer to involve large casts in the deployment of their plots, while the inept text is divided among many artists without rhyme nor reason, so that there is hardly any opportunity left for the individual actor to show off his skill. Besides, most plays are written in such a way that the actor has to go offstage from time to time, leaving the audience in the hands of mountebanks.

So what's left to the actor?

His exit!

There is nothing morbid about this word, it is no kin to the medical "exitus." It is an accepted term the world over, describing that breathtaking moment when the actor leaves the stage for a while and heads into the wings leaving in the consciousness of the spectators an almost physically painful void. The pain ceases only on the actor's hopefully prompt return and the audience expresses its deeply felt relief by spontaneous applause which speaks for itself. A good exit will always (except on feeble Mondays) squeeze out of the audience a dead certain storm of applause and on Saturdays at the second show, isolated ovations and loud bravos.

But the laws of exit are cruel: whether the audience bursts into spontaneous applause or not is decided only in that fateful instant when the actor leaves the stage. Planning ahead is about as effective as working out a roulette system. It's something fit to drive you mad.

Take for instance our Yarden Podmenitzki, who, according to all views, surpasses himself in the tyrant's burial scene. The audience listens spellbound, almost without coughing and chair-creaking, to his baneful funeral oration. He then steps in silent dignity toward the victory arch in front of curtain number two with three spots focused on him, and there he stops, and Mundek at the lighting console slides down on the rheostat and darkness gradually envelops the magnificent figure, and you feel the cheers in the air – Podmenitzki even manages a wan smile to underscore his inner pain – and *there is no applause*! Never. Why? I don't know. There just isn't. There is no applause. Podmenitzki claims that if they'd give him a simple line, a short sentence, just one word, he would bring the house down. But the director absolutely forbids him to add anything, even though he literally implores him to let him say just this: (*Bitterly*) "Riffraff!" (*Exit*).

On the other hand, Motke Shmulevitz always steals the show with his "nuts."

It is most upsetting. Everybody says that Shmulevitz is a proper disaster all through the show, but in the third act he has his moment of glory during his quarrel with the Cardinal. Gutman makes out of the Cardinal a sort of monster and the audience hates his guts right from the beginning, and then in the Inquisition torture chamber they have that quarrel, nothing special really, but before Shmulevitz is returned to his dungeon, the Cardinal asks him: (*Jeering.*) "Anything else, you heretic cur?"

At that point Shmulevitz, the devil, always takes a three-second breathing pause, lifts his right arm to make the chains on it jangle, and answers in a loud voice: "Nuts to you, Your Holiness!"

And exits.

The cheering sounds as if it will never end. Now that is an exit for you. Small wonder that I. L. Kunstatter wrote: "Mordechai Shmulevitz was at first a somewhat hesitant Mucius, but perked up toward the end."

Yes, such a "nuts" is a real dream. However, it's all a matter of chance. The playwright never makes allowances for a good exit; all he cares about is the success of his text, which is always lousy. Even worse is the director who literally sabotages the actor's exit because in his view "applause in the middle of a play only breaks up the rhythm of the show." Rhythm, you hear? Bullshit! This silly excuse is obviously rooted in envy pure and simple. Very frequently at rehearsals, you hear the director roaring from the stalls at a pitch bordering on rudeness: "Don't bow, goddam it, don't bow! I told you a million times: *out*, without any hocus pocus!"

Mrs. Kishinovskaya blinks in the klieg lights: "But I beg your pardon, I am just a silly, scared servant girl!" she shouts back at the top of her voice. "I've got to show respect for my mistress!"

"Don't show respect for her! You are an ignorant servant! *Carry on!*"

Mrs. Kishinovskaya, a veteran and well-disciplined actress, exits at all rehearsals without any hocus pocus, and only at the première does she bow right down to the floorboards – and gets no applause! However, at the Command Performance for the United Jewish Appeal Mission she adds a little improvised text, and while bowing, says: "It's because of women like you that we have inflation in this country!" and exits trembling and sobbing – the applause duly arrives!

To round out this theatrical success story, one ought to add that the author fell into a state of temporary stupor and complained about Mrs. Kishinovskaya to the management of the collective, but his complaint was rejected out of hand because Mrs. Kishinovskaya claimed that an actor is not a machine, but on the contrary sometimes a member of the collective management.

In any case, it should be clear now that the exit is a matter of initiative and intuition. In most cases the actor must see to it himself, in a clandestine manner, in view of the playwright's indifference and the director's sadism. The technique of the exit opens a wide field for verbal and movement improvisation. Here is a selection of proven exits with a 75 percent chance of cheers:

●Close the door slowly and quietly (possibly with a lone pistol shot offstage).

●Stop just short of the exit, turn around as if you wanted to add something else – a resigned wave of your hand – and out!

●As above, with satanic laughter.

●(*Softly*.): "Robert, I am in my fourth month." (*Drives off.*)

●Bent low and visibly heartbroken, walk with small steps toward the rear of the stage while the lights gradually fade (the tragedy of the little man).

●Mount the scaffold any old way.

●"Father!" (She has just discovered that he is her father.)

●Jump on somebody's back (male, or even better, female) and ride on him to the exit.

There is no limit to the possible variations. It is all decided in that fraction of a second. Old hands are able to raise quite satisfactory applause from a controlled limp or a fit of convulsive coughing. But after all is said and done, the best guarantee for a successful exit is still a bunch of relatives sitting in the orchestra.

HOW TO CUT LINES

First of all, let's define the concept "line." The actor has to speak certain sentences according to the script. The moment the director decides for some obscure reason to cut a sentence from the actor's part, it immediately becomes *the* line on which the whole play hinges. Therefore, it is every actor's sacred duty to fight like a wounded tiger every time the stupid director tries to exercise his despicable rights.

The length of the fight depends on the actor's importance and the review the director got from I. L. Kunstatter two months before. From Yarden Podmenitzki for instance, the hooligan took away *the* line of the play in the following way:

DIRECTOR: Just a sec! Podmenitzky, the train with mademoiselle is out! Check?

PODMENITZKI: Yes, sir, I see what you mean. Thank you, sir. (*Crosses out his line.*)

Now just for the record, let's see how this vital line is taken away from a more important actor.

DIRECTOR: Listen, Shmulik, I think your excellent entry would be even more effective if you would cut your "When does the train leave for St. Petersburg?" What do you say?

MORE IMPORTANT: As you like, I don't care. I belong to the old guard, if my director asks me to cut something, Shmuel Gutterman cuts. But for once I have the impression that from an emotional point of view it would be more soulful if I simply asked: "Waiting for the train, hey, Mademoiselle?"

DIRECTOR: All right. Say, "Train, what?" but in a whisper.

MORE IMPORTANT: As you like. (*Says it loudly.*)

Now we turn to the star.

DIRECTOR: Hold it, hold it! Excuse me folks for interrupting this marvelous rehearsal, but something happened to me, something quite unprecedented. When Mr. Finkelstein spoke his fantastic line: "Excuse me, Mademoiselle, when does the train leave for St. Petersburg?" I felt as if a fiery wheel were running down my spine and I was no longer able to concentrate, so overpowering was the effect. Shaul Finkelstein does not need me to mention here his pyramidal talent, his unbelievable intuition and his extraordinary impulsiveness, inborn qualities which give him a special status as the greatest actor of the last three generations, but it seems to me that we should not endanger the continuity of the show with such a powerful line, because there exists a real risk that the spectator will be as deeply moved as I was, or God forbid, could even suffer shock from the sheer voltage of his artistic enjoyment. Obviously, who am I and what am I to come here and tell Mr. Finkelstein what to say and what not to say in this play. I am only trying to make a small contribution in the form of a modest suggestion and I leave the final decision in the experienced hands of Mr. Finkelstein. Dear Mr. Finkelstein! After considering all the circumstances, do you too, think that it would be advisable to drop this line?

STAR: No. (*Everything stays as it was.*)

□ There is an erroneous belief that politics is the only profession whose practice necessitates neither education nor experience. This belief does not stand the test of reality, because there exists another profession, of a kindred nature, in which a person can become a hero of the gossip columns without any studies at all: acting. In order to correct this injustice and make it easier for the beginner actor to ruin himself, we concocted the following lesson after a particularly gruesome première.

WHO SAYS THERE ARE NO SMALL PARTS?

———□———

Young man, as you are about to take your first steps on the boards, which means the world, you are definitely entitled to the sympathy reserved for holy madmen. We shall pursue your career with vigilance and hope to see you in parts suited to your lively talent. However, since the nature of your parts might well determine your very future, we should like to give you some pertinent advice drawn straight from the Mediterranean repertory.

First of all, young artist, whenever possible, try to play in flops. In present-day Israeli theater you will find everything: glory, satisfaction, intrigue – everything except a way of making a living. It is no secret that your main income will be from side jobs, from publicity shorts, from dance routines at weddings, et cetera, but for all of these you need free evenings, and an actor who plays night after night in some miserable hit is in danger of starvation. Everyone gets rich on a hit: the theater, the playwright, the municipality – everyone except you the actor chained to your monthly salary. To say nothing of the fact that it is terribly boring to parrot the same lines night after night, in the same costume, on the same stage – why, it is practically an insult to your intelligence. Therefore, young artist, strive to appear only in bombs which get rave reviews. This is an ideal arrangement: to be praised by the press and then disappear quickly from the posters. In this connection we warmly recommend modern plays dealing with the lack of communication between man and man. They insure tremendous artistic achievement but also plenty of free evenings for side jobs. It's a dream.

It is also desirable, young chap, to appear often in classical plays written in verse and translated with stunning virtuosity by famous poets. In such plays there is always a part or two not written in rhyme, and should you succeed in grabbing such a part you will be the only actor on stage whose words are understood by the audience. Your clear and outstanding diction will be praised extravagantly in next morning's reviews. In the beginning also try to do a lot of Brecht, because your pallid acting will be interpreted by the experts as perfect Brechtian alienation. But for goodness' sake, stay away from any original play whose author is still alive, because the chances are that you won't succeed in "putting some life into such shadowy cardboard characters." An original play is a sort of domestic clash between the playwright and his reviewers. They have to come to some arrangement between themselves, and they don't need you for that.

So much for the play. Now about the part.

Stanislavski once said, "There are no small parts, only small-time actors." Maybe. It's a good idea to repeat this adage from time to time. All the same, take my advice: play only in big parts, huge parts, parts with lots and lots of text. That is the main thing, lots of talk, if possible alone onstage, or with the others just listening raptly to your words.

You should learn to read between the lines, young man. Before you start reading the play – naturally only those scenes in which you appear – take a well-sharpened red pencil and draw a circle around your speaking parts. In the end count the lines and check whether they are sufficiently numerous and whether they are buttressed by intoxicating blocks of monologue. Don't forget that no lesser authority than Comrade Lenin made the remark that quantity influences quality. If you have to choose between a big but trashy or a small but good part, by all means take the big trashy one because it will do you a lot of good. Believe me, great actors always play leading parts. That is why they are great. Should you ever see Sir Laurence Olivier play in *The Brothers Karamazov* anything but a brother or a Karamazov, you may change your outlook. Until then your motto should be: "There are no small parts, except those tailored for small-time actors."

Naturally, you should select with care the kind of parts you undertake to play. Never – you hear, never – take the part of a young, handsome, honest and rich man, who in addition – this is really too ridiculous for words – is head over heels in love. Such a part spells sudden death, a flop with an upper case "f." In real life one is either young or wealthy or beautiful or an actor, but one cannot impersonate all these up there on the stage without turning into something wooden and shallow, "a character who keeps alive onstage but does not bring the stage alive!" as the critics put it. Always play old people, young man, primitive and frightfully ugly folks, if possible with lots of weird perversions. At all events, note well the following: beauty is amateurish, ugliness is always artistic, poignant. All international prizes are automatically awarded to the impersonators of madmen, drunks and sundry sex offenders. These are the parts which give you a real chance to act. They have hair on their chests.

Here is another suggestion: try to acquire some sort of speech impediment, a little difficulty over certain letters, a slight stutter, or, best of all, a trace of hoarseness. This will make the audience identify very deeply with you. Normal speech sounds quite unnatural onstage. Similarly, rags are always more interesting than smart suits and an infirmity is incomparably superior to good health. Be sickly, young man, racked with disease. A slight limp the length of the stage insures you good reviews in most morning papers. A shaking deaf mute is certain to steal the show. A drug-addicted, drooling murderer who escapes from prison on a dark night automatically becomes an unforgettable character. More so if he secretly has a heart of gold. A drooling drug addict who escapes from prison on a dark night in order to adopt his victim's orphaned daughter – this part will catapult you right to the top of Mediterranean theater. Although it must be admitted that a drooling drug addict who escapes from prison, adopts the orphan and then rapes her near the footlights is quite likely to bring you a grant from some cultural foundation or other in recognition of your daring. A drooling drug addict who escapes from prison, adopts an orphan, rapes her on the spot and then surrenders to the authorities – such an outpouring of morality makes the awarding of the Tel Aviv Municipality Prize a foregone conclusion. And if the jury also finds you not guilty as they sympathize with you – the orphan really was a peach – and the outcome is a very happy end, you have excellent chances of getting a raise. Anyway, the future belongs to the monsters.

Always act the wretch, young man.

Nobody likes a big shot, everybody loves the underdog. Always choose the right profession, my boy. Whenever possible be the servant, not the master, a private and not an officer, a slave and not a slave driver. If you can manage it, try to be a Yemenite tea carrier. An old pickpocket is also excellent. A sad-eyed peddler is simply out of this world. But don't ever be a normal happy and healthy person unless you have definite masochistic tendencies.

And now, my young and promising friend, let's proceed to a dialectic analysis of your text. It is absolutely imperative that you never forget the following ironclad rules. Never ask questions onstage, always answer them. And look for parentheses because they mark the fat parts. Get the idea? Here, for instance, is an instructive passage from Schiller's *Mary Queen of Scots*:

MARY (*Drops to her knees softly.*):
    Indeed, the hour has come.
    Death, liberating and redeeming,
    Spread out your arms to receive me
OFFICER: And what shall I tell the Queen, Madam?
MARY (*Rises to her full height, proudly.*):
    To Elizabeth of England, give my sisterly

blessing. I pray that she forgive the
insults I heaped on her.

OFFICER: What else shall I say?

MARY (*With a subdued sob.*):
Tell her to forgive my death as
I forgive her with all my heart.

OFFICER: Is that all?

MARY: Since you ask, my man,
Tell my sister that I know she is but a tool
In the hands of forces greater than she.

OFFICER: What?

MARY: Goodbye, go in peace, good officer.
There is nothing left for me in this world.
(*Climbs scaffold steps with her head erect. Stormy applause.*)

Got the idea now? Never be an officer, young chap, always be Mary Queen of Scots. Let Stanislavski play the officer. Therefore, no questions onstage! And remember, the fellows who play parts sans parentheses always take the first curtain call. Lots of parentheses, lots of applause.

Naturally you should remember that most of the time you are not alone onstage and this is most unfortunate. Instead, you are hemmed in by masses of other actors thirsty for applause who could very well draw the audience's attention away from you. Therefore endeavor to play in productions with few characters. If ever you are offered a two-character play, don't even bother to read it – grab it. Another thing: never be on the same stage with children, because they are so much cuter than you and each of them has ten mamas in the audience. And never – you hear, never – play alongside scantily dressed females or Yemenite tea carriers.

The part makes or breaks the actor, believe me, young man. Therefore it is understandable that once the repertory committee decides on a play, a gigantic struggle ensues between the actors and the management which distributes quite indiscriminately those fat, questionless and parentheses-studded parts. In this situation the best advice is of no help whatsoever. Here everything depends on your personal valor, Mediterranean blackmailing powers and proneness to hysterics. For a good part, wage all-out war against the management, ring up the director at midnight, burst into tears, be violent, cough until you are blue in the face, bring them a letter from your psychoanalyst, convert to Islam – but don't accept a small part! Don't surrender to the management – fight it. As a matter of fact, why shouldn't you be in the management.

HOW TANGIER WAS SAVED

———— ☐ ————

Allow me to introduce myself: I'm making the Israeli action film *Where Eagles Fear to Tread*, one of the most daring adventures in the history of local cinema, written and directed by me, supported by foreign capital – that is, a Government advance. The plot is based on a real-life story from my imagination: an Israeli commando unit blows up the rocket base at Tangier and returns safely to the studio, which is rather tough on the actors because they've got to cross Egypt, Libya and Algeria on foot, but for that I'm paying them a fortune.

The first scenes went off without a hitch. The commander of the unit, Yarden Podmenitzki[1] in the part of gruff Grishka, picked his men from among some soldiers confined to barracks. He then led them through the Sahara – that is around and around Kibbutz Ein-Shahar in the Negev – for three days and three nights, till on the fourth day he finally arrived at my hut and came in and said: "Seems I've got to get back to Tel Aviv tomorrow."

"Are you out of your mind?" I said. "You're going to get

[1] Yarden Podmenitzki is not one of the giants of the Hebrew stage. On the other hand he is not a bad actor either. He is mediocre and that is really too bad, because he has ambitions of stardom without the star's inborn luck. He therefore builds himself a small ghetto in which he lives all by himself with his genius and the few acquaintances he succeeds in snaring off the street. Something else: he does not always play small parts. Sometimes he impersonates great personalities on the stage of very small theaters, moving every night to different locations.

ambushed tomorrow, remember?"

"Sorry," said Podmenitzki, "I had a call from the theater that there's a rehearsal tomorrow morning. We're doing *Hamlet* and I'm his father's ghost, a part I've been waiting for all my life."

"Do you know that's a breach of contract?"

"I'm sure it is, but I'm a member of a collective. Be hearing from you!"

And he left for the North. I decided to go on shooting according to plan and just add a bit of dialogue to explain the commander's sudden disappearance due to rehearsals. The dialogue took place between a sergeant called Tripoli and the wireless operator:

WIRELESS OPERATOR: "We're approaching Tangier. But I don't see Grishka. Where is he?"

TRIPOLI (*With an eloquent grin.*): "He'll be there, lad, you can rely on that."

You can't rely on anyone. Podmenitzki phoned that night to say that the collective had given him the part of the grandfather's ghost as well and that he had to write the text himself, so this week was out of the question.

"Podmenitzki," I told him curtly, "you're fired!"

He asked how much severance I'd pay, but I'd already hung up. The situation was delicate: the original plan had been for all my raiders to get back to base without any losses, but when I wrote the script I hadn't taken theater rehearsals into account. One thing was clear now: Grishka must die. As an artistic solution, I ordered a young vulture from the production manager. The vulture was to circle above him in the air and caw "Caw."

Podmenitzki's killing was reported by Tripoli in a brand-new scene. "They're going to pay dearly for Grishka!" said the sergeant, raising his hand in a fearsome oath. They trudged on through the desert without much difficulty, guided by the daughter of the Bedouin sheikh, Tsipi Weinstein, who had fallen in love with Grishka – that is, with Tripoli now. The raiding party crossed the Sahara, and as they arrived at the kibbutz exhausted but in fine fighting spirit, over the brow of the hill there appeared the figure of Grishka running and shouting: "Wait! The director's got a cold, I've got leave from the theater till Tuesday."

"Too bad, Podmenitzki," I yelled back. "We killed you yesterday. We've already ordered a vulture!"

However, since I'd hired him at a fixed sum for the entire film, it would have been a waste not to exploit him to the full. It was therefore decided that Podmenitzki would play ghost for us as well – that is, he'd float ahead of the unit to lead them through the desert, with organ accompaniment. Actually, he'd arrived just in time, as it seemed that Tripoli hadn't come back that morning from Eilat. Tripoli is a much-sought actor and participates, as a rule, in at least three films at once. In our case he was filming in Galilee from midnight on, then came to us at dawn and worked till noon, at which time a dusty jeep would rush up and grab him for American TV at Eilat until midnight. Now he'd vanished at some point midway – fallen asleep or something. At any rate, we had to go on without him. The medic of the commando unit, a cowherd by profession, whom we had loaned from the kibbutz for the duration, did the job.

"Boys," he declared in a close-up, "Tripoli is no more!"

"He covered our retreat," the unit commander added. "He fought to his last bullet."

Dammit, only now did I notice that I had been left without a unit commander. After Grishka's spiritualization, the unit had been left without a single name actor, except perhaps for Tsipi Weinstein, but she was the sheikh's daughter.

The new scene was very impressive: Tsipi stripped at dawn and informed the unit: "I'm a marine commando sergeant, I've taken over command!"

It was good to feel we hadn't been left leaderless for even a single yard, but we still needed to solve the problem of the father, the noble Bedouin sheikh himself. Therefore he too tore the *keffiyeh* off his head and introduced himself to the warriors: "Captain Lollik Tof of Jerusalem, counter-espionage. Follow me!"

All these momentous metamorphoses just for one Tripoli snoring away at some filling station somewhere between us and Eilat. Anyhow, the ranks were filled once more and the new captain strode lightly at the head of his unit beneath the burning desert sun. That evening the idiot had a fever: sunstroke.

"Malaria." I decided. "Carry him on a stretcher!"

The medic-cowherd and the wireless operator carried him for one full shooting day, and in the evening they told me that it was too much for them – the captain's heavy and he eats all day.

"Right," I said, "but what'll we do with him?"

The two of them lowered their eyes, then threw me a wordless look and I saw death in it. I agreed to the drastic solution. I gave the chief electrician a blanket and a stick; after all, he had been a Bedouin sheikh in the original text. He climbed a hill and in a marvelous distance shot he felled the captain with a single sniper's bullet.

The sergeant threw herself on her father's body. That is, she would have thrown herself if Tsipi could have been found.

"Miss Weinstein!" the production manager scurried through camp. "You've got a new scene on, Miss Weinstein!"

In a while the truth came to light: Tsipi had joined the Carmon folk dance troupe. I could feel it in my bones – she too wouldn't see another sun come up around here.

Tsipi fully deserved her punishment: she had got an offer from the well-known dance troupe and escaped from location to Haifa, to take part in the last two rehearsals before the troupe went off on a world tour. In my film she fell off the Red Rock. I couldn't show the actual falling because she was busy rehearsing in Haifa, as you will remember, so we only heard screams and the commando cowherd entered the tent and blurted: "She didn't suffer much. Her last words were . . . Tangier. . . ."

Here the wireless operator made a remark which in my view was cynical: that Tangier was located in Spain, with whom we maintained good relations. I threw an icy glance at this third-rate actor to whom I was paying ridiculously high daily wages, and saw him blanch. I did a beautiful funeral scene for wayward Tsipi, because funerals are the easiest thing in the movies – you can do them even without actors. Grishka's ghost delivered the eulogy I had written on my knee right there.

After Tsipi's funeral, Grishka took me aside. "I've been thinking of this part the whole time," he told me gravely. "Don't you think that from a purely dramatic viewpoint I ought to be buried beneath the desert sands, like some new Moses to whom it was not given to step. . . ."

"Podmenitzki," I said, "what's this about?"

"Sir," said Podmenitzki, "I feel like dying."

"Why?"

"My son is graduating from nursery school tomorrow morning at ten, and I promised I'd be there. Let me die tonight and I'll always remember you for it."

"Maybe you can tell me who's going to take Tangier if everybody dies on me?" I yelled. "I'll sue the lot of you!"

"The child," observed Podmenitzki, "has learned a poem by heart especially for the party."

"Drop dead!"

Which is just what happened: by force of circumstance Grishka's ghost stepped on a mine and died. After his sudden departure for the nursery school, I felt the blood go to my head, and a strange passion took me in its grip when my glance spotted the wireless-operator-on-daily-wages who had hidden himself, trembling all over, behind a rusty barrel. My eyes opened in an icy stare, and the wireless operator retreated to a far corner of the tent.

"No," he whispered, "you can't do that to me . . . I've got two days coming to me according to the contract . . . I'm still young, I want to live! Nooo . . . !"

I had him die of thirst in the heart of the desert. A gruesome death, but anyone who's going to quote trade union laws chapter and verse to me won't get any pity here. Only the commando cowherd was left now.

"Tangier!" In a low-angle shot he pointed at the kibbutz water tower and shouted to himself: "Follow me!"

At this point, within an inch of the conquest of the rocket base, we were rudely interrupted by the kibbutz secretariat. They stopped the commando cowherd in the middle of his lone charge and demanded that he get back to the cowshed on the double, as two cows with swollen bellies were expecting him.

"Gentlemen," I pleaded with the secretariat, "at least let him depart honorably!"

A snake bit him in the leg and I myself, dressed in the uniform of a U.N. officer, paid him final respects at the resplendent funeral rites attended, besides myself, by the kibbutz cook, who had a day off. I even added a couple of cannon volleys in the final mixing. It turned out quite an impressive occasion.

"They have fallen," I eulogized my contract-breaking actors, "but they knew what they wanted!"

On top of the hill Grishka's ghost stood at attention, because the kindergarten teacher had moved the party to the weekend. The vulture, high up in the air, summed up the whole matter with a few impressive caws.

While cutting the film I changed its title from *Where Eagles Fear to Tread* to *The Ghost Commando*. The U.N. officer, played by me, remained the main character in the film. A number of professional critics who viewed the first working copy cried like babies during the whole film. They said that the fact that not one of them makes it to the desired goal has a grim human documentary value which, notwithstanding a certain pacifistic tendency, is suffused with great humanitarian significance lending my work a universal appeal *par excellence*. They've got something there. I'd been thinking of that myself.

THE LEBERWURST CASE

———————□———————

O nce upon a time there was – and unfortunately there still is – a theater critic more of an ogre than any of his colleagues. People would open their newspapers after every premiere, holy awe in their souls, to find out whether they had liked the show or not. Because whatever I. L. Kunstatter wrote had the prestige of a divine decree. If Kunstatter wrote that the show was good, people flocked to the box office, except if it was a poor show not worth seeing. On the other hand, if Kunstatter wrote that the show was – oy – bad, nothing could help that show, except if it was a good show worth seeing. And that's how it went for dozens of years: the critic criticized, the theaters trembled in their every board and the playwrights choked on their bile and scribbled inept little attacks against Kunstatter, which were just flashes in the pan.

However, one evening a momentous event occurred.

Kunstatter sat down to his gourmet dinner, during the course of which he tasted a piece of fresh leberwurst manufactured by Leberwurst and Son Ltd. He had barely taken a bite of it when he spat it out in a flat parabola and remarked to his wife, Mrs. Kunstatter: "This is leberwurst? This is dried cow dung! I'll give it such a write-up they won't forget it to their dying day!" Kunstatter is a man of deeds, so he sat down at his desk and wrote a poisonous review headed "A Disgusting National Scandal Which Smells To Heaven!" and worded as follows: "In the last few days, our country's defenseless citizenry has been choking on that nauseating centipede which its criminal manufac- turers for some reason dare to call leberwurst." Kunstatter wrote this after cautiously deleting some more pungent expressions. "Only criminals lacking any decency and moved by the most despicable motives of gain are capable of throwing onto the market such disgusting slaughterhouse offal. We feel certain that our consumers, blessed with proverbial good taste, will indignantly and definitely boycott this unpalatable garbage, phooey."

Kunstatter immediately summoned a messenger and sent the review to his paper which automatically printed it the next day – and with that it seemed that the affair had ended. However, things did not quite work out that way. Leberwurst and Son Ltd. sued the surprised critic. The press naturally played up the case and the leberwurst trial hit the headlines. The country promptly split into two camps: one of them claimed that Kunstatter had every right in the world to pan the product mercilessly if he really had not liked it since this was a matter of free press and the only relevant question was: did we, or did we not believe in the critic's fairness and honesty? On the other hand, there were those who had tasted the leberwurst and found it excellent. There was also a small group which approved of the review itself, but rejected its moderate and lukewarm style. In short, there was a big to-do.

I. L. Kunstatter himself lectured on the subject at the artists' club: "Infamous leberwurst," he shouted from the rostrum, his face livid, "stinking leberwurst, stupid leberwurst, worthless leberwurst, rotten leberwurst, stale leberwurst, scandalous leberwurst, a leberwurst which is not even leberwurst!"

After this sensational lecture, Kunstatter was escorted home by plainclothes men. He had become the country's most famous man. Tickets to his trial were sold at premium prices. As his interrogation started, tension in court reached fever pitch.

JUDGE: Mr. Kunstatter, do you plead guilty?

KUNSTATTER: Never! What's more, I'm sorry I didn't use stronger terms to describe this . . . (struck from the record).

JUDGE: Why did you write the review?

KUNSTATTER: Because this was my view!

JUDGE: Are you an expert?

KUNSTATTER: Yes! For the past twenty years I've been eating leberwurst regularly.

JUDGE: Are you also familiar with the production process?

KUNSTATTER: That is quite irrelevant! The process can be faultless and the product – if Your Honor will excuse the expression – . . .

(*struck from the record*).

JUDGE: If you had found the leberwurst tasty, would you also have reviewed it?

KUNSTATTER: Why write about an acceptable leberwurst?

Counsel representing Leberwurst and Son Ltd. asked the defendant at this point whether he had consulted other people before panning the leberwurst? Following the arrogantly negative reply, the prosecution summoned a number of witnesses. They tasted the leberwurst exhibited on the Judge's bench and declared that it was quite good.

KUNSTATTER: A completely amateurish attitude! "Coca-Cola" is a fantastic success all over the world and yet it is pure hogwash.

JUDGE: This is your private view, if I'm not mistaken?

KUNSTATTER: Of course it's my private view! I cannot eat and drink with other people's mouths! Everything is individual. Quite possibly, this leberwurst may be tasty to everybody else, but me it makes sick!

JUDGE: Are you ready to declare this on oath, Mr. Kunstatter?

KUNSTATTER: Willingly!

The irate critic places his right hand on the Bible and declares in a loud and categorical voice that "this leberwurst is an inferior and despicable, degenerate and incompatible product which maliciously taints the state's nutritional standards." The great oath sounded so convincing that even Kunstatter's rivals had to admit that the critic gave the impression of an honest man ready to die rather than be deflected from a cause he considered just. After this, it was assumed that Kunstatter would earn a full acquittal. While the court retired to consider its verdict, his many well-wishers thronged around, congratulating him on his brilliant moral victory. I. L. Kunstatter sat quietly in the dock, a serene smile of self-confidence playing on his lips.

The court gave the critic, for libelous slander and causing serious commercial loss, a two years' suspended sentence and a fine of Sh.15,000. "Nowhere in the world," to quote from the decision, "does the law empower a citizen publicly to voice his subjective views as to whether a certain leberwurst is good or not, since the expression of such views could cause losses to the factory producing that leberwurst. Only the taste of the general public may decide the degree to which a leberwurst is palatable or otherwise. If every private citizen were given the right to influence the public from the pages of the newspapers according to his personal likes and dislikes, an absurd situation would be created leading unavoidably to the bankruptcy of the leberwurst industry. . . ."

Kunstatter appealed the sentence. The suit "Coca-Cola" filed against him is due to be heard next week. So far, the sausage crisis has not been resolved. But ever since, Kunstatter no longer roasts leberwurst. He reserves his poison for theatrical performances.

THE ART OF GETTING
A RAVE NOTICE

———☐———

"Look, the premiere ended only ten minutes ago, and there is I. L. Kunstatter running for the phone to dictate his review. Again he'll be the only critic to make the morning papers."

"Are you worried?"

"Not at all. He'll give us a fantastic review."

"Are you sure?"

"One hundred percent."

"Is the show that good?"

"What show?"

"Your show, the show Kunstatter is going to review."

"What has the show got to do with the review?"

"I thought that . . . after all. . . ."

"Don't be ridiculous. The times are long past when a theater manager like myself could rely on the excellence of his productions. Nowadays, in the age of guided criticism, it's only ice-cold reasoning that counts."

"For instance?"

"For instance, the choice of play. Why do you think I chose a Polish drama from the thirteenth century?"

"Because Kunstatter . . . ?"

"Right. Because Kunstatter is Chairman of the Israel–Poland Friendship Council."

"I see. That should rate you a special review."

"Not necessarily. Now and again he has to prove to his readers that, although he is Chairman of the Council, he is quite objective toward Polish art, and then he is ruthless."

"So why aren't you worried now?"

"Because I did not trust to blind luck. I waited patiently until two months ago, when Kunstatter tore to shreds the Polish dance group which visited the country, and then I said to the boys: 'Now we can come out with a Polish play without any danger from him.' "

"That sounds easy."

"It only sounds so. Nowadays a good review depends on thousands of small details. After all, Kunstatter could conceivably praise the play to the skies and yet completely demolish the production."

"So what could you do against that?"

"I apply the well-tested roulette system. I watch out for a succession of five blacks, then bet on red – and get away with the show. See?"

"No."

"See this little notebook? Here I write down whatever Kunstatter has said about other premieres during the last few months. Here: on May 23, 1987 – 'a minor horror'; on June 7, 1987 – 'a slapdash job'; on June 19, 1987 – 'how much longer?': – on June 30, 1987 – 'obnoxious clowning': on July 6, 1987 – 'a miserable farce.' Five times black; now, according to the laws of roulette, the sixth time he is bound to write a good review, otherwise they'd suspect him of bitterness. I expect to get at least 'plastic, highly expressive acting, creating good rapport with the audience' out of him."

"Quite a job."

"We have ordered a small computer for next season, but for the time being I have to handle things by myself. In any case, the direction and decor will earn Kunstatter's fullest praise."

"How do you know?"

"We are linked to Plotkin."

"Come again?"

"I always try to come out right after Gershon Plotkin's premiere at the Chamber Theater. Now, everybody knows that Kunstatter hates Plotkin like the plague because Plotkin once said that he was dumpy. Ever since, Kunstatter has automatically slaughtered Plotkin's directing. That's only natural. However, Kunstatter knows that while Plotkin is used to the harsh words about his directing, he will absolutely blow his top if, in the same paper, side by side with his being slaughtered, he reads kudos for the director of another show running at the same time. So I always come out with our new production close on the heels of Plotkin. That ensures unreserved superlatives for our directors. As a rule, whenever Kunstatter is complimenting someone, he's trying to annoy someone else."

"You said the decor will also get praise?"

"Yes. Here we deal from a position of strength. Six weeks ago, the father of our stage designer, himself a well-known sculptor, boxed Kunstatter's ears because of some sort of art review. The incident was widely reported in the press and now Kunstatter has no alternative but to praise the daughter's work, otherwise people will say he's just being spiteful."

"What a lucky break that her father should have beaten him up just at the right time!"

"Luck doesn't come into this at all. He did it on my instructions. 'You want your daughter to get good reviews?' I asked him. 'Then bash in Kunstatter's head.' Believe me, it's not at all easy to coordinate all these factors. Take the casting, for instance. I gave the lead to an actor who is mediocre, Yarden Podmenitzki, and thereby had the benefit of a doubt."

"What doubt?"

"The publisher who publishes Kunstatter's collected reviews year after year is also named Podmenitzki."

"I see: he's related to the actor."

"Not at all. But Kunstatter is under the impression that he is. After all, it's a rather uncommon name. So Podmenitzki always steals the show with him. Here, see what my notebook says: April 3, 1985 – 'I

was surprised by Podmenitzki's refreshing playing'; August 11, 1986 –
'The surprise of the evening was Podmenitzki . . .'; February 27, 1987 –
'To our pleasant surprise, Podmenitzki.' Before this premiere, just to
play it safe, I sent Podmenitzki to ambush Kunstatter in front of the
publisher's office. They bumped into each other on the staircase, the
actor going up, the critic coming down. At a cautious estimate this
should guarantee Podmenitzki a 'subtle, well-balanced and amazing
performance.' "

"I can see you've thought of everybody."

"Not of everybody. That would be a fatal mistake. You always
have to leave a weak link in the chain on which the critic can vent his
ire. If you don't plan for that in advance, he could hurt something really
valuable. So better hand him his victim on a platter. In our show, for
instance, the lightning rod is the composer of the music."

"How does that work, if I may ask?"

"Very simple: I looked for a composer of Hungarian origin. As
you know, Kunstatter is allergic to Hungarians, for hereditary reasons.
So the music of our composer will be 'anemic, raucous and utterly alien
to the spirit of our country!' The poor guy will absorb the whole
quantity of unavoidable bile.

"I take my hat off to you, sir."

"I haven't finished yet. You have to think of the smallest details.
The show was ready to go way back in June, but I held up the premiere
until the humidity had dropped somewhat, because it has a marked
influence on him. Above 85 percent he is merciless, that's a well-
known fact. Everything is under control. I have also surrounded his
seat with a steel ring of actors' relations, and to tickle him pink even
before the curtain rose, I seated his keenest competitor, the critic S.
Greenbotater, three rows behind him, right on the aisle."

"Just a second. So what's Greenbotater going to write?"

"Don't be funny, he translated the play!"

"Perfect planning, I must say."

"It has to be perfect. More than sixty theater people work
months on end on such a play, so I can't take chances when so much is

at stake. Every show deserves professional protection, and so does a beauty like ours. Are you going to see it?"

"I think I will."

"When?"

"I don't know yet. I'm waiting to see the reviews."

Science has invented measuring apparatus for everything. We have instruments for measuring the intensity of ultraviolet radiation, the variations in humidity, the success of nuclear tests. Only for social success there is no measuring gadget. That is, there is one. And it's homemade.

YOU CAN'T FOOL MENASHE

—————□—————

One of those wet evenings we were again sitting, Ervinke and I, at our café command post, watching the flotsam and jetsam flowing between the tables. Suddenly the writer Tola'at Shani plowed his way toward us and started biting his nails.

"I'm terribly nervous," he confessed. "Right now the Repertory Committee is deciding the fate of my play."

We sympathized with him. If they rejected the play, all was lost. On the other hand, if they accepted it the possibility of its reaching the stage by mistake need not be ruled out altogether. We tried to calm the poet, but he was tense to distraction, and from time to time broke into hysterical giggles and threatened to emigrate.

Then something strange happened. A tall, lean man who passed our table and greeted Ervinke with a light wave of his hand stopped in front of Tola'at Shani, raised his head, his nostrils trembling, his face contorted with a superhuman effort. This lasted for a fraction of a second, then the man relaxed, raised a languid finger and threw an icy "Hi!" at Tola'at Shani. Then his noble figure was swallowed up in the thick smoke blanketing the café.

"Sorry, Tola'at Shani," Ervinke said sadly. "The Repertory Committee has rejected your play. Unanimously, I'm afraid."

The poet shuddered and gripped the edge of the table.

"But . . . how do you . . . know?"

"From the successometer," Ervinke said, motioning in the

91

general direction of the tall man. "Menashe never errs."

"Menashe is a genius at societymanship," Ervinke explained. "He always sticks to successful people and shuns them like the plague once their star begins to fade. As far as I am concerned, Menashe is a perfect one-man Gallup poll. From the way he greets me I know with dead certainty what my social standing is at any given moment."

Suddenly I also remembered. Of course! Only a few years ago the man never failed to slap me on the back whenever he passed our table. Once, if I remember rightly, it was after the State Department had invited me to the U.S. No, come to think of it, it was the day before the invitation came through. He actually sat down and inquired about my health.

"Menashe is a born barometer," Ervinke continued. "His nervous system resembles a sensitive radar network. He registers the slightest social tremors, any wisp of success, any achievement, any intimation of failure – and treats his acquaintances accordingly. Whoever gets a loud and hearty 'Shalom' from him can be quite certain that he is on top at the moment. Those with checkered careers get a cursory wave of the finger and sometimes, when an artist gets a particularly murderous review in the press, or someone goes bankrupt, Menashe gives him a subsonic hello which hardly registers even on the most sensitive listening devices.

"And the most fantastic part of it is," Ervinke went on, "the successometer does not necessarily react only to current status. He is liable to hug a writer who has only recently been crucified on the pages of the literary supplements because his electronic brain has already sensed a future box-office success, or a prize in the offing, or a legacy. He has an uncanny ability to make snap decisions on the success coefficient of the person he is meeting. See what I mean?"

"No."

"I'll give you an example," said Ervinke. "The moment Menashe caught sight of Tola'at Shani, the little wheels in his brain started spinning. 'A poet of uncertain employment,' the transistors flashed.

'I'll give him the standard No. 8 greeting – "How are you, boy?" – medium volume, and what's more, since the critic Birnbaum mentioned his collected poems two days ago, I'll slow down as I pass his table.' On the other hand, since Kunstatter the Great has not invited Tola'at Shani to his table for the past two weeks (and besides the writer's son has a bad cold), Menashe drops the too cordial 'boy.' However, it is well known that Mrs. Tola'at Shani has a rich uncle in Brooklyn, so Menashe turns on a fairly friendly grin and lifts three fingers during the 'How are you.' That was the successometer's reckoning, but at the last moment Menashe registered a supersensory message concerning the Repertory Committee's decision to reject the play. This automatically canceled the friendly grin, the 'How are you' was replaced by a nine-below-zero 'Hi' and even that with only one finger raised to barely hip height.

"From that I knew," Ervinke continued, "that the play had been rejected unanimously. Had there been *any* votes in favor, Menashe would have raised two fingers shoulder-high."

As Ervinke finished his lecture, the theater manager came towards us.

"Disaster!" he informed Tola'at Shani. "They all voted against the play."

At midnight, after we had dragged Tola'at Shani's ghost into a taxi, Menashe appeared in the café doorway and made a beeline for Ervinke. He pinched my friend's cheek and said in a clear voice, grinning broadly, "Say, where have you been these last few days?"

The broad grin lasted for one–two–three–four whole seconds! Ervinke grew deathly pale, ran to the nearest lottery stand and checked the list of winners. Then he broke into cheers. He had won 4,000 shekels.

"Only one thing I don't understand," Ervinke mused after he had calmed down somewhat. "Why did Menashe not kiss me? Above three thousand shekels he always kisses. Hopp!" He slapped his forehead. "I forgot – I owe sixteen hundred shekels!"

As we left, I gave Menashe a particularly cheerful "Good night." He looked through me at the night horizon as if I simply were not there. What's the matter? What's . . . the matter . . . ?

□ *It appears that our economy is making unprecedentedly large strides. While other countries of our comic size need a consolidation process extending over a dozen years in order to reach the peak of economic prosperity, we, notwithstanding our crippling war expenses, find ourselves after just a few years already on the way down toward economic stagnation. But whoever thinks this is a terrible tragedy apparently cannot stand on his head. In other words, without that skill it is a little hard to find your financial legs in our country.*

A YOUNG PERSON'S
GUIDE TO FINANCIAL
INDEPENDENCE

———□———

It is no longer a secret that the possibilities for earning easy money are becoming ever more restricted. The stringent security measures taken all over our country have cut down the frequency of diamond robberies to not more than one a week, and even here there is a waiting list to the end of the next fiscal year. So the only feasible short cut to a consolidation of the individual's economic situation is bankruptcy.

PREPARATIONS. Naturally, not everyone can go bankrupt at the drop of a hat. The act demands careful preparation and great astuteness in the moment of truth. The first step in launching a bankruptcy is the establishment of a company with a ringing foreign name. The company may deal in imports, show business or haberdashery – it makes no difference as long as it is of limited liability, hereinafter Ltd. "Liability" means that somebody is liable, while "limited" hints at the fact that it is not us. Personally, we only manage the company on its way to the scheduled bankruptcy. We sign contracts, take advances, order merchandise all over the world, request subsidies and are indefatigable. In return for these managerial services we allocate ourselves large salaries, fat bonuses, lavish expense accounts and business trips to the Bahamas. The wife also is employed with the company as deputy-bankrupt and purchases the company car for Sh.50 in easy installments.

However, people are not that gullible. Before they grant credits to a Ltd., they check whether the company has any money in the bank. It has! How come? Simple: we lend our Ltd. a certain sum of money out of our own pockets and put it in the bank where everybody can see it.

Then we go bankrupt.

This, as a matter of fact, is inevitable. Because of our huge overdrafts, the company loses its pants, and one somber day the creditors of the Ltd. meet and start playing cards with the company's bounced checks. Then there follow six rather difficult months for the little bankrupt, chock-full of threats, telephone calls, broken window-panes and last warnings by nervous lawyers.

This period has to be borne patiently.

THE TURNING POINT. Some time before the turning point we go to the bank and withdraw back into our pockets the loan we advanced the company. Down to the last agora. Then we convene our creditors for a national convention in the Philharmonic Auditorium and address them in the following terms: "Friends, I have gone bankrupt! I fought hard, I made sacrifices, I tried, but they broke me. This is a lousy country, taxes, terrific taxes. It's altogether impossible to make a living. My company hasn't got an agora to its name, only debts. This is the end. Now that I've told you the truth I feel better. Thanks for your attention."

The creditors sit all around us in the spacious concert hall and their eyes are as glassy as a masterpiece by Benvenuto Cellini, the illustrious son of Florence. They know they cannot do a thing, because it is not we who owe them money but fate – that is, the Ltd. – and after all, what can you expect from three letters? Deepest despondency reigns within the hall.

"However," we suddenly say, "however, dear friends, if you'll let me continue, if you'll give me a little breathing space, say for a month or two years, then maybe, one of these days, who knows but I may repay all the company's debts down to the last agora."

The creditors say, "Will you excuse us?" and go into a huddle in the restaurant around the corner. It doesn't take them long to realize that they have no choice. If they allow the Ltd. to declare itself officially bankrupt, they won't ever see a shekel of their money, because its remaining assets will be siphoned off by the multitude of official receivers, while the bankrupt, his property safely restored, will be free as a bird, looking for new adventures. Besides, it is most unpleasant to write down in the books: "This investment turned into shit." Banks are especially reluctant to have to explain to the Comptroller checking their balance sheets: "Well, yes, this money is written off." And just between ourselves, what is there to lose? As long as the debt exists, there is at least a glimmer of hope.

The creditors' reply is therefore, "O.K., carry on!"

Here we crawl out from under the table, purple in the face.

"Carry on?" we shout in a towering rage. "Perhaps you can tell me how. How, damn it, can you ask a man to take upon himself the management of a ruined company whose safe is completely empty? You are ridiculous, so help me!"

There and then the hat is passed around and the result is Sh.400 in cash and Sh.3,600 in promissory notes.

THE PAMPERING. In the nature of things, the Hebrew creditor is fated to chase his money until his last breath. The Ltd. manager is therefore extended new credit on condition that he does not declare himself an official bankrupt and instead continues his duties as head of the company. Then starts a marvelous period of pampering and pleasantness. It is almost incredible what one can squeeze out of an Israeli creditor whose back is to the wall. It is related that Avital Sulzbaum, the king of bankrupts, last winter made his creditors at the bankruptcy meeting drop to their knees and worship him before he graciously agreed to continue in office.

"Good Lord," the hosts of creditors prayed, "please, please keep him in good health!"

Anxious souls have been known to send their family doctor to the bankrupt, naturally at their own expense. They see to it that his sex life is well regulated, provide masseurs, etc. They slip him pocket money as well as subscription tickets to the Philharmonic. In short, they keep him swaddled in cotton wool. The creditors organize a "Sulzbaum Club" whose registered aim is to safeguard the bankrupt manager's work capacity. It is a wonderful feeling to know that one is beloved and cherished. It is said that frequently the principal creditor has his daughter marry the bankrupt in order to insure his money. Or else he names him his legal heir. As a rule, creditors also provide a guard of honor wherever he goes.

This is a very cozy situation, this popularity, this *dolce vita*. And the moment discipline slackens or snide remarks are dropped, it is enough to raise your voice a few notches.

"As a matter of fact, what do I need this for? I'll declare myself bankrupt and be done with it!"

The collection is resumed right away, unreserved homage paid. They have no choice; we are in a position of strength because we are bankrupt.

THE DANGER. It sometimes happens that the bankrupt loses control over his life's work and under the influence of alcohol or in a fit of momentary recklessness starts repaying the company debts to the creditors. As long as payment is in the order of Sh. 200 a year, there is nothing to be afraid of; on the contrary, this keeps up the tension. But should he foolishly repay the whole debt, he is lost. It is well nigh impossible to describe the seething fury of the Mediterranean creditor who has received all his money back. We know of a sad case where one of the Ltd.'s government grants was, through a clerical error, transferred to a principal creditor. The man pocketed the money and then went and beat up the bankrupt.

A manager who pays up exposes himself to attack like a turtle which rashly crawls out of its shell. His fate is the fate of the ordinary honest person; all he gets is kicks and abuse. Therefore it is vital to maintain a preventive debt to the end of his days, as this is the key to a comfortable and carefree existence.

THE CRUCIAL QUESTION. Readers might be tempted to ask themselves the question: since this sounds so easy, why doesn't everybody go bankrupt?

Who says they don't?

□ *There are plenty of ways for a government to turn its citizens into crooks: frequent devaluations, for instance, which keep nibbling at the citizen's savings; sky-high income tax as a punishment for hard work and talent; and best of all, keeping strict control over foreign currency in circulation. Our Labor government was particularly good at that: for the 40 years of its reign it forbade the citizen to keep any foreign currency at all – at home or in the bank – except if the citizen could prove that he intended to squander it all abroad to the last shekel. The result was inevitable: a great flourishing of the black market and of ESP.*

INSPECTOR FISHBAUM'S ESP

———□———

It was blind chance that revealed the extraordinary powers of Inspector Hanaya Fishbaum of ITI (Income Tax Intelligence).

It all started when one Freddy Mizrahi, a tractor wholesaler, declared the sum of Sh.413 as being his annual income for 1980/1, while at the same time buying up the odd side of Yarkon Street and a pair of trained dolphins.

Tipped off by an unidentified source, the ITI started collecting information about Mizrahi. It laid on a couple of detectives to tail the tractors, got in touch with Interpol, consulted a psychologist, and kept feeding its own giant computer with the incoming data. Eventually their efforts bore fruit: ITI concluded that Mizrahi was concealing part of his income.

The ITI squad, under the personal command of Inspector H. Fishbaum, launched its raid on the suspect's lavish apartment at 5:05 A.M. sharp. Swift and efficient as ever, they made straight for the wardrobe and came up with 20,000 Swiss francs, and secret accounts showing concealed profits of Sh.340,000 a month.

With his eyes boring through the top button of Mizrahi's

pajamas, Inspector Fishbaum said, "Sh.413 – ha?"

"Please," said the trembling Mizrahi, "please, I was about to come clean. I meant to call on the tax office this very morning and . . . ."

"No kidding," said Fishbaum sarcastically. "I bet all your tractors together couldn't have dragged you there, Mr. Mizrahi!"

"I haven't got any tractors," whispered the man, "and my name is Beanstock."

Well, to err is human. The squad had pounced on the wrong wardrobe. Fishbaum ordered his men to arrest Beanstock. He then asked him where Mr. Mizrahi lived. But Beanstock had fainted, so Fishbaum rang next door and an elderly woman opened.

"Sorry about the early hour," the inspector apologized. "We're from the ITI, and we wanted to ask where. . . ."

The woman screamed once and rushed into the bedroom.

"Shmuel!" she yelled. "They're here! The checkbooks! Quick!"

By the time our gallant squad reached the bedroom they found that Shmuel had swallowed three checkbooks of a respectable foreign bank and the key of the safe, which they only just managed to salvage because it had stuck in his throat. Shmuel's D-Marks turned up between "Laches" and "Lox" in the Jewish Encyclopedia, and Mrs. Shmuel, who just stood there mumbling, "I told you so, Shmuel, I told you we'd have to declare *something*. . . ." turned out to have $30 in her hair by way of rollers.

"Book 'em!" said Fishbaum, and leapt nimbly up the stairs to the third floor, where he found the Mizrahi apartment by looking at the names on the doors.

Tricky to the last, the tractor man tried to evade arrest by hanging himself in the bathroom, but they cut him down. They discovered his books in the freezer, and after thawing them out perceived his annual income to be not Sh.413, as stated, but Sh.12 million. Next they removed a wobbly tile in the kitchen and hit upon 15 pounds of enriched uranium. There's serendipity for you.

Mizrahi was detained, his apartment locked, and Fishbaum went in search of the janitor to hand over the keys.

"I'm Fishbaum from ITI," he introduced himself to the janitor, "I've come to hand. . . . No!"

But he needn't have worried. The janitor landed on the grass when he jumped out of the window and only twisted an ankle. And although he had dumped his 30,000 yen in the john, he hadn't had time to pull the chain. His lodger had been too busy hiding the gold in the jam jar to help.

At 7:30 that morning the squad returned in triumphal procession to Headquarters with five tax evaders in tow, a bagful of loot, and plenty of data for the computer. . . .

Thus started the wondrous career of Inspector Hanaya "Goldfinger" Fishbaum.

The news of his sensational talent for catching tax offenders spread like wildfire through the Treasury. Some people argued that the fact that he'd nabbed all the culprits in one building must have been pure accident, but events soon proved that nothing more nor less was involved than a plain and straightforward supernatural phenomenon.

Take the case of the three Drs. Bluebottle.

Informer No. 181,302 had put the ITI onto a Dr. Bluebottle, but had been unable to supply any further details about him. The computer disgorged three potential tax evaders of that name, and Headquarters were sitting with their hands in their hair when somebody remembered Fishbaum. Of course!

They wrote down the addresses of the three Bluebottles – a lawyer, a gynecologist, and a garage mechanic – and handed the list to Fishbaum. Fishbaum stared at it, concentrated hard for one long suspenseful minute, and then his (gold) finger shot out and jabbed the address of the mechanic. To be brief, the man turned out to have a concealed income of Sh. 3 million, a sheer platinum bathtub, and a few dozen diamonds stuck in a cake of soap.

Fishbaum has become a legend in his lifetime. It is said that he can open the phone book, go into a light trance, run his finger slowly down the page, and stop suddenly at a name. The commando unit goes out and never returns empty-handed.

Because Fishbaum has never been wrong. Not once!

Even the parapsychologists are stunned by his uncanny powers. What really gets them is the fact that Fishbaum's ESP is actually improving with time. For instance, he no longer needs written lists. He just sits still and meditates a while with his eyes closed, then jumps up and announces, "So-and-so of Rehovot, of such-and-such a street, such-and-such number, third floor, first door to the right!" He's never wrong. Last week he suddenly pointed at a passer-by in the street and cried, "Catch him! He's a tax fiddler!" The man broke down there and then and confessed all.

Fishbaum's superiors at ITI don't know *what* to do to hold on to their miracle man. They're afraid he'll quit one day soon and go over to the private sector. It'll cost them a fortune, because while he may still be willing to put his sixth sense at their disposal, he'll demand the regular informer's fee of 10 percent like everybody else. He need squeal on only half the population to become a mutimillionaire within the year.

It follows that just now, H. G. Fishbaum is the most pampered civil servant alive. Only the other day they gave him a special award on behalf of the Min. of Fin., a medal with Uri Geller's head on one side and 100 percent marginal tax on the other.

OPERATION BABEL

———————□———————

It started with my having to transact a small deal involving X-ray apparatus. I called at the Allopathic Trade Ministry, intending to inquire whether you could get a license[1] for the import of X-ray apparatus donated by your relatives abroad if, even though you were not a doctor, you suffered from bulbous duodenitis and therefore had to X-ray your stomach at frequent intervals.

Everything went smoothly at the Ministry. The inquiry booth was staffed by a young man deputizing for his uncle (just then on reserve service) who tentatively sent me to Room 1203, from where I was rerouted to Room 4.

Passing through Rooms 17, 3, 2004, 81 and 95, I reached Room 504, which was the office of a Dr. Bar Cyanide, Counselor Without Portfolio for X-ray Affairs. There was not a soul in front of his door, but I was informed that you could enter the room only if you were in possession of a little slip of paper with a number on it. This was to prevent the forming of awkward lines.[2] Numbers were distributed in Room 18.

There was a terrific line in front of Room 18, and I calculated that at the rate of one person every thirty seconds, plus an exceptional case after every third simple one, my turn would not come in under five or

[1] We inherited many good things from the Mandatory Government, but a fondness for licenses is not one of them. Anybody who wants to import or export cars, refrigerators, food, books, flowers, brushes, or needles must apply for a special license. By the time the license is issued, the refrigerator has melted in the sun, the food spoiled, the book flopped, and the needle buried itself in a haystack. That is why the official issuing the license has to be prodded.

[2] Far be it from me to try to lecture the reader on standing in lines. We Israelis consider the line a necessary evil, but in Britain the "queue" is considered a way of life. Our only ambition is to jump the line (even our ancestor Jacob received the paternal blessing out of turn), so all our sympathy goes to the Briton who calmly, patiently and conscientiously stands in the bus line for hours and only starts pushing and shoving when the bus pulls up.

six years, which is a very long time even in the present difficult economic conditions.

As there had always been a base and selfish streak in my character, I entered the adjoining Room 17, and through it insolently penetrated into Room 18, where they were distributing the line-avoiding numbers.

Just then there were no customers in the room, only a burly basilisk-eyed official who, startled by my unexpected entrance, bawled me out in the following words: "No entering from the side! I won't receive you! Didn't you see the line outside? You have to join it just like everybody else!"[3]

On such occasions, you have to come up with something unusual, otherwise you are sunk.

"Bulbous" – I stressed the name of my disease – "bulbous duodenitis."

The official was a medical ignoramaus. He stared at me, utterly bewildered.

[3] We Israelis are green with envy when we think of the polite manners one finds in offices all over the Western hemisphere. Here in Israel a typical phone conversation with the average secretary of a government official goes somewhat like this:

We: Is Mr. X in his office?

She: Are you kidding?

We: When is he supposed to be back?

She: How should I know?

We: Would you mind taking a message for Mr. X?

She: Have you gone out of your mind? (Replaces the receiver without having written down a single word.)

Whereas in the civilized West:

We: Is Mr. X in his office?

She: I'm afraid he isn't, sir.

We: When is he supposed to be back?

She: I'm awfully sorry, but I'm afraid I can't tell you, sir. The weather is pleasant today, isn't it?

We: Rather. The rain was much warmer these last few days. Would you mind taking a message for Mr. X?

She: Not at all, sir.

(We slowly dictate the message, spelling the more difficult words.)

She: Thank you very much, sir. Goodbye, sir. (Replaces receiver without having written down a single word.)

"What?" he said. "Who? Why?"

And then I had a brain wave, which I think could revolutionize standing in line in Israel.

"*Dvargichoke plokay gvichkir?*" I asked the official, smiling amiably. "*Shimusek groggy. Latiten?*"[4]

That floored him.

"*Redste* Yiddish?" he asked. "*Efsher redste* you speak English?"

"*Dvargichoke plokay.*"

"*Redste Fransoa?*"

"*Gvichkir u mugvichkir.*"

The official rose and called in a cashier from the adjoining room.

"This poor devil speaks only Hungarian," he said to his colleague. "You are from Transylvania. Perhaps you could ask him what on earth he wants.

"*Haver,*" the cashier addressed me, "*te mit akarol mama?*"

"*Dvargichoke plokay,*" I promptly answered. "*Latiten?*"

The cashier next tried Romanian and Carpatho-Ruthenian, then shrugged his shoulder and left me to my fate. A sallow-complexioned clerk of the Calorie Computing Department came down from the third floor and quizzed me in Arabic, Turkish and Dutch. I naturally stuck to my *dvargichokes* and spread my arms in regret. Then came an engineer from the second floor, and we quickly ran through the Slavic languages. Nothing.

The tea carrier happened to speak Finnish. "*Shmusek,*" I repeated desperately. "*Shmusek groggy!*" A counselor with a B.A. tried Latin, then the Director General of the Rice Control Section addressed me in Rhaeto-Romanic. "*Gvichkir.*" An unknown woman babbled something in Italian, Spanish and Japanese, then they called up the gatekeeper, an immigrant from Afghanistan, who addressed me in his native tongue and in broken Abyssinian.

By the time a cannibalistic pygmy bookkeeper was trying his luck with the language of the Gnu-gnu tribe, quite a crowd had gathered

---

[4] To avoid any misunderstanding, this is pure gibberish, not Hebrew.

around me, and all were trying to guess where I came from and what it was I wanted.

The cashiers swore to my being a mestizo White Indian, while the others inclined toward taking me for an Eskimo, but this was categorically denied by the Director of the East European Desk, himself an Eskimo.

Alerted by telephone, the Controller of Vanishing Stocks tried to clear up things in Malay, but ran into a solid wall of *dvargichokes*. Came the Coordinator of Public Delusions with Aramaic. "*Plokay*." Walloon, Basque. "*Mugvichkir*." Norwegian, Papuan, Greek, Portuguese, Tibetan, Ladino, Swaheli, Latvian, Volapùk. . . . Nothing. Not a word.

When everybody was lying completely exhausted at my feet, I strolled over to the official's desk, and as if I had just discovered them, picked up one of the numbers scattered all over it. (Remember? That's what I had come for in the first place.)

"He wants a number!" The good news spread like wildfire through the dark corridors. "A number is what he wants! Finally! A number! Hallelujah!"

The officials forced another number on me, patted me on the back, congratulated me, embraced me, and I think the Controller even kissed the fringe of my coat. . . . Eyes were moist. . . . People were marveling at the Ingathering of the Exiles. (Later I found another dozen numbers in my pockets.)

"*Dvella*," I mumbled, slightly moved myself. "*Dvella*."

□ *Insurance is one of the greatest mysteries of modern life. The initial process is fairly smooth: the agent comes, jabbers, we say no, the wife says yes, we sign the microscopic print (Para. 302, page 14 of the policy, at bottom: "The insured party declares hereby that he relinquishes any claim for payment of damages promised to him in this policy. This relinquishment is final and irrevocable.") Then you have some accident, the assessor comes, takes notes, and it turns out you only get 15 percent of the damages because it happened on a Wednesday. At this point the Jewish genius enters the picture.*

INSURED INCOME

The other night I'm just about to drive my car out of the parking lot when a well-dressed citizen comes up to me and says: "Excuse me, but I think that if you back out now you'll smash my fender."

I looked at the huge American car parked obliquely behind me. "O.K." I said. "I'll watch out."

"Not at all," said the well-dressed citizen, "I would *like* you to smash my fender. I'm collecting bodywork."

I left my car, and by the light of the pale moon received a basic lesson from the citizen. He pointed at the bashed-in roof of his car.

"A traffic light collided with me," he explained. "I've shown it to Zion, my favorite bodyman, but Zion told me: 'It's not worth your while repairing this, Dr. Wechsler, because the insurance won't pay for it. Why don't you collect a few more knocks and come back then.'"

We sat down on the fender in question.

"There's a clause in every policy that says the insured party has to pay for the first Sh. 230 of the damage," my pal explained. "The repair and painting of my roof would only come to Sh. 200, so it's not worth my while to put in a claim. On the other hand, if I could get another few decent knocks. . . ."

"Just a second, Dr. Wechsler," I interrupted. "Even if you completely destroy all your fenders, you'll still have to pay the first Sh.230."

"Sir," Wechsler assured me, "leave that to Zion."

That's how I was introduced to Zionism – I mean to the fact that there's a secret agreement between the International Organization of Bodyworkers and the Car Owners Union in Copenhagen, whereby the world's tinsmiths present the insurance companies with bills padded by Sh.230. Still, for that you have to collect knocks to the tune of at least Sh.1,500, so that your own contribution will be swallowed inconspicuously in Zion's bill. He, my pal that is, was considered an old hand in the trade. Once he'd collected Sh.2,800 damage in just under two days.

"And now here I am stuck with this stupid roof," Wechsler poured out his distress. "I've been running all over town for weeks trying to get another couple of knocks, but in vain. Believe me, I've tried everything. I pull up suddenly in front of trucks, I overtake buses, park next to military vehicles, and yet now when I need it in a hurry, nobody hits me. I'm simply out of luck. So I thought that if you could kindly back into my fender. . . ."

"With pleasure," I answered, "it's the least I can do."

I went into reverse and started out toward the fender.

"Hold it!" Wechsler shouted. "What sort of driving is that? Step on the gas or you won't even make Sh.60."

I went back to my starting point, pushed the accelerator down to the floor and whammed my bumper straight into his body. It gave a very satisfactory crunch.

"O.K?"

"Not bad," said Wechsler appraisingly, "but that's not more than six or seven hundred shekels. The insurance won't give it more. Back in the good old days when you only had to pay the first Sh.110, you could make do with a fender job. Now you've literally got to demolish your car. Would you mind doing the door?"

"Sure."

I guess this is what they mean by "driver solidarity." There's something admirable about a man helping his fellows, like when a strange car pulls up at the roadside and asks, "Can I help you, lady?"

"Shoot!"

I gave myself a good long run, jammed down the accelerator once more and rocketed into my target. Zzing! Glass splinters flew and Dr. Wechsler's door fell off its hinges, completely buckled. There's something to this, so help me.

"Another go?"

I was quite ready to complete the job. It occurred to me you could even go professional: a sideshow at the fair called "Collect Bodywork!" Buy a ticket and join the fun. The customer speeds into a car set up for the purpose and the damage goes up on an insurance scoreboard in colored lights. Sh.1,000 – 1,500 – 3,000!!

"Thanks, that'll do," my new friend said. "I think I'm all right now."

I was a little disappointed but, after all, it was his car.

I made another check of the damage I had inflicted. Good! With the sense of a job well done I returned to my own car and found the grille over the bumper all crumpled up.

"So sorry," Dr. Wechsler apologized, "but you're obviously still a beginner. Where bodywork is concerned you always want to hit from the on-side. Well, a new grille won't cost you more than Sh.50. With your permission I'll add another Sh.400."

That sounded reasonable. Wechsler revved up his American monster and hit my left door with great feeling.

"You still want a headlight."

He gave my headlight an expert swipe.

"That's it," my pal said. "Look in on Zion tomorrow, you won't have to pay a penny."

My eyes were burning and my hands itched in a funny sort of way. I proposed to Wechsler that we put some distance between our two cars and then rush straight at each other, bonnet to bonnet. It must be an interesting experience to see your car turn into junk before your eyes. . . .

"Don't overdo it, sir," Dr. Wechsler calmed me. "This thing shouldn't become a habit. The moment your insurance is covered – stop!"

He was right. We parted with a friendly handshake.

Wechsler went to see Zion and I bought myself a new car.

POOR NO MORE

———☐———

"Mr. Sallah Shabati? May I?"

"Yeah, come on in, mister. You can sit on that busted case in the corner there."

"Thank you."

"If the kids are in the way I can strangle them."

"No, it's all right."

"Fine, then I'll just lock them up in the bathroom. You from a daily or a weekly?"

"A daily."

"Friday supplement?"

"Yes, Mr. Shabati. I saw your ad in the paper yesterday: 'Slum fam. with 13 chil. at the disposal of the media.' Could you give me some time now?"

"An hour and a half. I did two radio interviews this morning, and I fixed with the television at three, but right now we can talk some."

"Thank you, Mr. Shabati. Well then, my first question. . . ."

"Hold it, hold it. What's the pay?"

"What's the what?"

"Na, mister, you figure I live in this hovel on 1,130 shekels a month just for the heck of it? Social distress is pretty hot on the market these days, so a man wants to cash in on it. Look, if you do a nice feature with lots of squalor and all, then your paper's circulation goes up, and I bet your own salary won't suffer either, right? Not to mention your reputation as a reporter with a social conscience. I give a real stirring description, mister, with heaps of embitterment. . . ."

"All right, how much do you want?"

"My usual is 300 shekels an hour, including VAT. Add 30 percent if it's with pictures. Cash. No checks."

"You mean 324 shekels an hour?"

"I still got to pay my publicity agent out of that too. That's the rate, mister. Maybe around the Yemenite Quarter you'll find distress for 100 shekels, but you get stuff to fit – 11 kids at most, nearly all of them fat, and 1,659 shekels a month. Me, I give you 19 heads in a space of 55 square meters, with three grandmothers. . . ."

"Where's your wife?"

"Getting photographed on the roof, pregnant, hanging diapers on the antenna."

"Don't you get any welfare?"

"I waived it, mister. Got to keep up my standing on the squalor market. Write-ups pay a deal better. Next February I'm moving into a dovecote for a TV documentary. I'll take in a goat too. Where's your photographer?"

"He's on his way."

"I want a two-page spread with a three-inch caption."

"Don't worry, Mr. Shabati, we'll do the right thing by you."

"Fine, so start writing, mister."

"My first question is: do you feel frustrated, Mr. Shabati?"

"Why should I? I'm real grateful to the Israeli public. It's got a heart of gold. Sure, they don't exactly knock themselves out to eliminate poverty, and no one cares about what goes on in the slums of his own city, except they got this law encouraging every poor sod to have ten children. On the other hand, though, the nice people aren't half cut up every time our misery is exposed on TV. It's sure inspiring. All those professors and sociologists talking so grim. Anyhow, what with distress being so big with the media, the demand for in-depth features has gone up, and the economic standard of us underprivileged has improved no end. You know, mister, I guess this is the first country in the world that's solving its poverty problems through interviews. . . ."

□ *The favorite fruit of our well-irrigated country is the* melon, *since the water supply of our melon patches does not depend on the clouds' good will, but rather on the prompt payment of water bills. The only disadvantage of the melon is Tsuriel, the Oriental fruit hawker. His one eye squints to the right, the other to the left, and the third looks you straight in the eye.*

WHAT'S IN A MELON?

————□————

DR. FEINHOLZ (*Passes fruit market on his way home and remembers that his wife Elisabeth always forgets to bring home watermelons, although it is summer and the heat almost unbearable. Walks to the mountain of melons towering in the middle of the market and speaks to Tsuriel, who is the creator and owner of the mountain.*): Are they sweet?

TSURIEL (*Does not answer.*)

DR. FEINHOLZ: All right, give me one.

TSURIEL (*His X-ray glance sweeps over the green hills surrounding him, he picks up a particularly swollen melon, tosses it in the air, catches it, paws it, squeezes it, raps it, looks at its stem, raises it to his ear, and throws it back. Takes another one – air . . . squeeze . . . rap . . . stem . . . ear . . . away. Third one is all right. Weighs it with back to customer, in the darkest corner of the market.*): Six kilos. Seventy-seven agorot.

DR. FEINHOLZ: Is it sweet?

TSURIEL: Sweet.

DR. FEINHOLZ: How do you know?

TSURIEL: Experience.

DR. FEINHOLZ: What experience?

TSURIEL: I feel it in my bones. A melon which is not quite ripe goes "plopp." One that is ripe goes "plopp."

DR. FEINHOLZ: I see. (*Pays, and in the asphalt-melting heat lugs home the five-kilo melon. On way understands why wife always forgets to bring*

115

watermelons. At home he puts melon in refrigerator. At end of meal, as a pleasant surprise, takes it out and cuts it open.)

WATERMELON (*Yellow, tastes like frozen rubber sponge. Was probably watered with kerosene.*)

DR. FEINHOLZ (*Spits out melon. Angry*): That's Israel for you! And I paid seventy-seven agorot!

ELISABETH: Take it back!

DR. FEINHOLZ: Right you are. There's a limit even to my patience. (*In the broiling heat drags back the monstrosity and hurls it at Tsuriel's feet.*) Hey, what's this?

TSURIEL (*Does not answer.*)

DR. FEINHOLZ: It's uneatable, that's what it is.

TSURIEL: Then don't eat it.

DR. FEINHOLZ: But you said it was sweet.

TSURIEL: It plopped all right. But who knows what you did with it at home?

DR. FEINHOLZ: Now look here, don't you think you are responsible for your melons?

TSURIEL: No.

DR. FEINHOLZ: How come?

TSURIEL: Did you buy it with a guarantee?

DR. FEINHOLZ: What's the difference?

TSURIEL: Without guarantee it costs twelve agorot the kilo, with guarantee eighteen agorot. Then I'm responsible. Completely.

DR. FEINHOLZ (*Points at the yellow mass at his feet.*): And what about this?

TSURIEL: Got any chickens at home?

DR. FEINHOLZ (*Disgusted. Kicks melon.*): All right, give me one with a guarantee. But it had better be good, or else. . . .

TSURIEL (*Tosses one in the air, paws it, squeezes it, raps it, looks at its stem, lifts it to his ear, throws it away. Same with second melon. Third is all right.*): Seven kilos eighty.

DR. FEINHOLZ: O.K.

TSURIEL (*Cuts out three-ounce slice from melon and shows it to Dr. Feinholz.*): Red?

DR. FEINHOLZ: Red.

TSURIEL: I don't like to brag, but this is a really red, red melon.

DR. FEINHOLZ (*Pays, then, sweating and groaning, carries the six kilos home.*): The old so-and-so exchanged it without a word of protest.

ELISABETH: Naturally.

DR. FEINHOLZ (*Puts the treasure in the refrigerator, waits for about half an hour, then takes it out and cuts it open.*): Now this is red, isn't it?

ELISABETH: Have you tasted it?

DR. FEINHOLZ: I haven't tasted it, but – I guarantee, my dear.

WATERMELON (*Is sallow, senile, sour, stale, sodden and even sniggers.*)

ELISABETH: Take it nicely back, will you?

DR. FEINHOLZ: Course. (*Furnace. Sweat. Lug. Toss.*) What's this?

TSURIEL (*Does not answer.*)

DR. FEINHOLZ: Did I buy it with your guarantee or didn't I?

TSURIEL: You bought it.

DR. FEINHOLZ: Then taste it.

TSURIEL: Thanks, but I don't like melons. They make me perspire.

DR. FEINHOLZ: You call this sweet? Where is this sweet?

TSURIEL: I didn't guarantee sweetness. I only guaranteed that it would be red.

DR. FEINHOLZ: I don't give a damn about the color. For all I care it could be topaz blue.

TSURIEL: Then why didn't you tell me that the taste also mattered? The guarantee for sweetness costs twenty-one agorot a kilo.

DR. FEINHOLZ: All right, give me one!

TSURIEL (*Up, paw, squeeze, pat, stem, ear, away. Second. Third.*): Nine kilos thirty.

DR. FEINHOLZ: Just a moment! I want to taste it.

TSURIEL: As you like. (*Cuts out a pyramidal wedge in such a way that the tip of the pyramid comes from the geometric center of the melon.*)

DR. FEINHOLZ (*Bites off tip*): Now this really is sweet, my good man.

TSURIEL (*Quickly replaces wedge in melon.*): Two shekels ten.

DR. FEINHOLZ (*Pays and staggers home.*): I had him exchange it, darling.

Now taste this!

ELISABETH (*Tastes it, spits.*)

WATERMELON (*Completely tasteless, dishwater. Wherever one looks — seeds. One inch from center turns into pumpkin.*)

ELISABETH: Take it back!

DR. FEINHOLZ (*Groans, leaves.*): What's this?

TSURIEL (*Does not answer.*)

TSURIEL: You tasted it, no?

DR. FEINHOLZ: What I tasted was sweet.

TSURIEL: Then what? Here it's sweet and at home it's sour? What are you doing with these melons at home? Pickling them?

DR. FEINHOLZ (*Asthmatic coughing mixed with Teutonic cuss words.*)

TSURIEL (*Slaps his client's back*): You want another?

DR. FEINHOLZ: Yes!

TSURIEL (*Picks up one, tosses it in the air, squeezes it.*)

DR. FEINHOLZ: Squeeze your grandmother, you crook! I'll pick my own!

TSURIEL: Please.

DR. FEINHOLZ (*Picks a bottle-green one, taps its side and at that moment a queer tingling in his subconscious makes him feel dead certain that this melon just has to be sweet. We are in the presence of a mysterious, awe-inspiring instinct.*)

TSURIEL: Sixteen kilos eighty. You want my guarantee?

DR. FEINHOLZ: Drop dead. (*Groan. Home.*) Had him change it.

ELISABETH: I see.

DR. FEINHOLZ (*Puts melon in freezer and crawls in after it. Waits for a few minutes, but it is very cold, so he cuts melon open.*)

WATERMELON (*Sweet, red, crisp, export quality, tender, dewy, delicate and without a single seed.*)

DR. FEINHOLZ (*Pops out of freezer. Life is beautiful. Little birds are singing in the trees.*): Taste this! Upon my word, that fool tried three times and missed, while I, led by some demoniac instinct. . . .

ELISABETH: Nonsense.

DR. FEINHOLZ: Nonsense? I'll show you! (*Next day again picks his own melon, again feels that inexplicable, subconscious prompting. Pays. Groans. Freezer. Out. Cut.*)

WATERMELON (*Rotting and awful. Jeers at gullible humans.*)

DR. FEINHOLZ (*Tries to blow out his brains. Poor marksmanship saves his life.*)

☐ *Tourism is the world's best business, especially in a country where only the time differential prevented Moses, Jesus and Mohammed from holding a symposium on the subject "Monotheism and Its Influence on the Flow of Tourists." In line with this concept we have a special ministry for the encouragement of tourism, which patiently explains to the population that we have to handle our foreign guests with exceptional courtesy, even though this may cause some discomfort here and there. As a matter of fact, the courtesy business has not yet quite come off, but the discomfort has been fully implemented.*

THE TOURIST BLITZ

———————☐———————

Humidity. They say it's mainly the humidity which drives them to the cooler North. They crawl around, sweating and sticky, through Tel Aviv's narrow, steaming alleyways, and the only thing which keeps them alive is the thought of the marvelous weekend they will spend on the shores of Kinneret. So we booked a double room at the largest hotel in Tiberias and sighed, greatly relieved.

We arrived at our destination in excellent spirits, knowing that the above establishment is the exclusive spa's most exclusive inn, its rooms spacious, deeply cooled and sybaritically comfortable. In short, we prepared to feel like kings for a day.

But we sensed a certain coolness in the manner of the clerk at the reception desk.

"Sorry," he apologized on behalf of the management, "sorry, but a group of tourists from the Winegrowers' Conference are due at our hotel, so we cannot offer you, sir or ma'am, a room except in the old wing, and even that cubbyhole has to be vacated by noon tomorrow, unless you don't mind being thrown out bodily. We are sure you understand our difficult position, sir."

"I protest," I protested. "My money is as good as the tourists', isn't it?"

"Who's talking about money?" the desk cut us short. "It is our patriotic duty to make the stay of these tourists as pleasant as possible. Besides, they give bigger tips. So get moving, but quick!"

We hurried down to the old wing so as not to give him a pretext for kicking us out. After all, desk is desk and not just plain anybody. Our little room was somewhat stuffy, but good enough for the natives. We unpacked, then with springy, careless steps sauntered off for a Kinneret swim. One of the deputy managers intercepted us.

"Why are you hanging about here?" He frowned at us. "The tourists are due any moment. Back to your kennels!"

We drew in our tails and hurried back to base, but by then a sentry had been placed in front of our door. It appears that tourists from the Peashooter Congress were also due. Our luggage had been moved to the nether regions, next to the boiler room.

"You can stay here until eleven," said the sentry, who at heart was a decent chap, "but don't use the hot water, the tourists need it."

By then we dared move through the corridors only by hugging the walls, and a deep inferiority complex had gripped us.

"Do you think they'll flog us or something?" the wife whispered, but I assured her that as long as we cooperated with the desk we were not in any immediate physical danger. Only once did we see some sort of manager patrolling the Israeli quarters with a cat-o'-nine-tails, but we carefully avoided him. After lunch we had a nap on our pallet, but were awakened by the din of an arriving motorized column. We peeped out through a crack in the wall and saw about a dozen luxurious buses, each containing a complete conference. We made a quick appraisal of the situation. I called the desk.

"To the sub-basement?"

"At the double!"

We moved down to the oubliettes. It was quite pleasant, except for the bats. The dinner tray was slipped under our door. Ready for all eventualities, we did not undress, expecting more tourists to arrive.

And indeed, at midnight they moved us again, this time onto a raft on the lake. Actually, we were lucky to get an almost new raft. The other hapless natives got just a few planks and logs.

Three drowned. Fortunately, the tourists didn't notice.

☐ *If, for technical reasons, the immigrant to Israel cannot become a doctor, a career with the civil service is the second-best bet. The Israeli official's salary is rather low, but he enjoys frequent tea breaks and may therefore be considered an intellectual.*

The most striking trait of the Israeli official is that he is simply not there. Or rather he is there all right, but not at the office. Officials are always in conferences. There are thousands of pretexts for holding conferences. Some conferences drag on for two or three days, others last only five or six hours. In the meantime, one has to wait.

A METEORIC CAREER

———☐———

One hot summer day my father-in-law Bernhard, a veteran Zionist worker who came to Israel not long ago, received a recommendation[1] addressed to the Amidar Housing Corporation, asking them to allot him a flat, and not to charge him more than the usual price, if possible. So off I went myself to Amidar's head office to get the matter settled. I climbed the stairs to Room 314 looking for Mr. Heshvan, who takes care of these things.

In Room 314 not a living soul was to be seen. I asked someone in the next room, and they told me that Mr. Heshvan was in conference with Mr. Stern, but he was due to come back any moment now. "Take a seat, sir, take a seat."

Well, there I was taking a seat and getting up and sitting down again in Room 314 when in came a man who asked, "Where's Heshvan?" Said I, "He's in conference with Stern. Take a seat."

---

[1] While the State is unable to give every new immigrant an apartment, it does, however, reward veteran Zionist militants in this way, with the logical consequences that everybody is a veteran Zionist militant. There are so far fifty officially registered former secretaries of Theodor Herzl.

The man was in a hurry and disappeared, and a few minutes later some sort of official came in and looked around the room. "Don't get excited," I told him. "Heshvan is with Stern. He's due to come back here any minute. Take a seat."

"Thanks," he said. "When Heshvan comes in, tell him he's to come straightaway for a conference with Mayer."

"O.K." I said.

In a little while in came another official, a plump one, and he asked, "Where's Kirschner?"

"He was here a minute ago," I replied. "If Heshvan comes back from Stern I'll send him along straightaway. Take a seat."

"O.K." said the plump chap. "You don't know if he's managed to tackle the Ramat Aron Housing Plan?"

"Very likely," said I.

"Then I'll take the files with me. If he wants Feintuch, tell him I'm in conference with Mayer."

What do you think happened next? A few seconds later Kirschner came back at the run. "Where's the Ramat Aron file? The old man will get wild again if it isn't found straightaway."

"Heavens above!" I shouted at Kirschner. "Just this minute Feintuch took it off to the Old Man's conference!"

"And where's Heshvan?"

"He's still with Stern. I'm waiting for him, too."

"O.K." said Kirschner. "If that's how it is, would you mind sticking these plans from Goldberg into the Giv'at Seren file?"

"Certainly," I replied. I went up to the filing cabinet, found the Giv'at Seren file after a brief search, and added Goldberg's plans. Suddenly Feintuch burst into the room.

"Good God!" I exclaimed, losing my temper. "Why aren't you at the conference yet? The Old Man's in a terrible state – do you want another explosion?"

"I'm on my way. I just came for Goldberg's plans."

"Is this a time to come, Feintuch, when I've already put them in with the Giv'at Seren file?" I cried. "Now I'll have to look for them all over again. Everybody takes advantage of me, and I, like a fool, let them do it."

Feintuch dithered for a moment in obvious confusion. "I've only just been told that Mayer wants them," he stuttered apologetically. "What do you think of the plans?"

"Not bad" was my verdict. "Anyway, I'd like to know what the Old Man will say."

Feintuch took the plans off with him for Mayer, but before he went out he said the Old Man would like me to look over the list of tenants in the Shekem Housing Project and submit a report to Stern. I went to work without delay and began to examine the list with great care.

A minute or two later in came Feintuch – Mayer wanted to see me straightaway. "I've only one pair of hands!" I complained, and off I went to see the Old Man. Mayer wanted to hear my opinion on the quality of the building work in Ramat Aron. I told him frankly that the houses were too close together and the windows too small. Kirschner began to stammer that it was the usual thing.

"What do I care if it's usual?" I said. "Things can't go on this way!"

The Old Man said I was a hundred percent right, and immediately sent Kirschner packing (Now – I thought – he'll hate me!) and told me to go ahead and deal with the Ramat Aron file. Straightaway I sent for Feintuch and instructed him to give me a report within twenty-four hours. Then I rang up the information desk, ordered a car, and went out to the site. I exchanged a few words with the foreman, examined the plans, made a few minor improvements, and fired an insolent engineer without severance pay.

When I came back to the office, they were waiting for me in great excitement. Kirschner had begun to whisper behind my back, because he was jealous of my meteoric career. I could see from the corner of my eye that he went pale as a ghost when Feintuch came running in to say that Stern himself wanted me to come to a most urgent conference. I submitted to Stern a detailed oral report on the progress of the building operation, and he criticized the slow pace of the work.

"Now look here, Stern," I said. "Without authority I can't do a thing!"

Stern accepted my point of view, immediately summoned an extraordinary meeting, and announced to the staff he had appointed me his deputy. Mayer began to throw out hints about the short time I had been in the service, but Stern had already got used to these intrigues against me, and in closing the meeting he demonstratively pressed my hand and encouraged me to carry on.

I rushed back to my room to have another quick glance at the problem of Giv'at Seren. There I found a new face. Mayer introduced him to me – it was Mr. Heshvan. I entrusted him with an important task in registration, then told him: "I'm not a monster, but I demand accuracy and punctuality, and I insist particularly that during the hours when the office is open to the public the staff of my department should not take part in conferences. This practice is liable to give rise to the most peculiar situations."

Next I allocated my father-in-law a complete block of flats in Ramat Gan and drew an advance on my salary. Ever since then I have been working in the Amidar offices. I receive the public from 11 A.M. to 1 P.M., Room 314. If you don't find me in my room, you will know I am in conference – take a seat, sir, take a seat.

THE BRILLIANT CAREER
OF PROFESSOR HONIG

———————□———————

D r. Immanuel Walter Honig was born in Frankfurt-am-Main about sixty years ago. He graduated from high school in Prague, then studied mathematics at the University of Antwerp. His parents urged him to study real estate brokerage, but the young man threw himself with single-minded devotion into the natural sciences and obtained his Ph.D. at the Sorbonne and his M.Sc. (Econ.) at the University of Basel.

By then Dr. Honig was thirty-five, because a bout of TB, caused by the protracted burning of midnight oil, had forced him to lay off his studies for a while.

After his recovery, Dr. Honig took postgraduate training in political science, and at forty became an assistant lecturer at Oxford. As a result of another five years of strenuous scientific work, he became the director of Rome's State High School. During this fertile period Professor Honig wrote his thirteen-volume masterpiece *Effects of Economic Index Fluctuations on the Sociological Development of the Middle Classes*. At fifty Dr. Honig realized the dream of a lifetime and came to Israel with his family.

The professor settled down in a modest housing development near Tel Aviv. His family consisted of his wife Emma, two children, his father, mother-in-law and father-in-law. Dr. Honig was immediately employed by one of the most distinguished secondary schools and for a while lived without worries. His colleagues paid the brilliant scholar the respect that was his due, and in his spare time he developed a new theory on the computing of the life-expectancy coefficient in insurance work.

The situation deteriorated in the summer of 1976. Certain material shortcomings made themselves felt in the professor's budget.

Life was becoming more expensive by leaps and bounds, and providing for such a large family became a Herculean task. The scientist had to give up buying the books he needed for his research. In 1978 the professor's situation had become well-nigh untenable, although he frequently walked to school and fasted once a week.

To illustrate Dr. Honig's critical situation, we reproduce the following chart[1] of his income:

YEAR	GROSS MONTHLY SALARY (shekels)	NET INCOME (shekels)	REMARKS
1976	2,537.00	2,014.53	–
1977	2,926.50	1,965.03	*Mrs. Honig got herself a job*[2]
1978	3,254.95	1,968.70	*Salary rise after hunger strike*[3]

Gradually Dr. Honig sold all his valuables, and one day reached the stage when he had nothing more to sell, except perhaps his elderly relatives. In the end Emma took a desperate step and fired off a letter to a New York uncle whom she loathed. The letter pulled at the

[1] To understand the chart, the reader must be given a number of intimate details on the working of Israeli income tax. The Jews, cruelly oppressed for two thousand years, became used in the Diaspora to hostile authorities' trying to steal their property under the guise of collecting taxes. Now that we have a State, the Jews still go on evading taxes and fail to understand the all-important difference that now it is not hostile goys but good Jews who are trying to fleece them under the guise of tax-collecting. The result of this is that every Jew declares only half of what he really earns. So the authorities double their demands. And thus things get settled nicely. Except for the poor devils who – misunderstanding the authorities' true intentions – declare their full income. One of these was Dr. I. W. Honig.

[2] A clever trick of the income tax authorities, according to which if husband and wife are both working, they have to pay more taxes. This is the spirit of the East, which, as the reader probably remembers, is greatly opposed to having women work . . . for wages.

[3] From time to time, the eggheads strike for higher salaries (instead of growing larger families. What decadence!). In the end they win a small raise, thereby come into a higher tax bracket, and find that $2 + 1 = 1$.

heartstrings of the American uncle, who immediately dispatched twenty large bars of chocolate in a big parcel. What else could the professor do? He sold the parcel to the school janitor, who felt it to be his vocation to sell sweets to studious youth.

And then what did the playful Fates do? They whispered in Professor Honig's ear that the crooked janitor had sold for 20 shekels the chocolate he had bought for 5 shekels.

But where was the justice of it all, the professor wondered, and he quickly had Emma write another letter to the uncle. Three months later another parcel arrived, but the professor did not again put its contents at the disposal of the janitor; instead, he peddled the chocolate among the pupils at Sh. 1·20 a bar.[4] The windfall balanced the professor's budget and thereby definitely mellowed his outlook on the fluctuations of the economic index.

"Why only American parcels?" the professor mused, and he began selling his pupils local products as well. Dr. Honig did this in a quiet and unobtrusive way. After each lesson he pulled out a small tray

[4] No reason to feel ashamed! Once, employees lived merely on their salaries; now, thanks to the wealth of taxes, loans, duties, levies, new customs duties, and other blessings, people have to work more, produce more, in other words look for other sources of income to complement their thoroughly diminished salaries.

Here then are the results of a private Gallup poll on the leisure pastimes of key salaried people living in our midst:

R.L., prominent municipal engineer. Sells lottery tickets to contractors. His wife mends stockings without telling the income tax authorities. In lunch breaks sings on Kol Yisrael radio.

K.N., cashier, 37 years on the job. Works until midnight as acrobat, from midnight until 8 A.M. as night watchman. Sends word he has flu and knits pullovers at home. Also embezzles.

A.P., high-school Bible teacher. Works as aircraft spray pilot in the afternoon. Received Sh.100 for his tenth child. Sold two sons and a daughter to the missionaries. Dances at weddings. Studies safecracking.

T.A., high Treasury official (Grade 8). Works evenings as bus boy. Saturdays and holidays gives skateboard lessons. Removes and sells light bulbs from his office. During vacations: espionage for a foreign power.

S.P., world-famous actor. Mornings works as cook in a Jaffa joint. After shows asks loans from critics. Takes collars off dogs roaming the streets and sells them.

from under his desk and addressed the pupils as follows: "Chocolate, waffles, cookies. Sour candies, peppermints, toffee. Caramels, chewing gum – export quality."

The pupils responded. The sale of sweets proved a reliable source of income, and Dr. Honig's living standard began rising in a steep curve. Early in 1980 he dropped his weekly fast day and went to work by bus. In 1981 he could afford an occasional visit to the cinema, and lately he has begun to put on some weight. His depression has vanished and he can again devote himself to scientific research. The not quite unjustified inferiority complex with which the professor was afflicted in the past has been completely sublimated, and he now faces society as a man whose position and dignity are certainly not below those of bus drivers and building contractors.

Below is a chart reflecting Dr. Honig's income derived from the sale of candy-industry products.

YEAR	GROSS MONTHLY TAKE (shekels)	NET INCOME (shekels)	REMARKS
1981	3,423.00	3,423.00	–
1982	3,510.00	3,510.00	*Introduced ice cream*
1983	6,078.95	6,078.95	*Introduced hamburgers*

Some time ago a regrettable incident threatened to mar Dr. Honig's upward-arching career. The school management objected to Professor Honig's custom of roaming the school corridors with a tray hanging on his neck. It warned him that such behavior could not be reconciled with pedagogical ethics.

Naturally, Dr. Honig immediately tendered his resignation. Since then he has made his living exclusively from the sale of sweets. He even went into partnership with the janitor, the institute's former English literature teacher.

Today Dr. Immanuel Walter Honig is an established citizen.

Some time ago he moved into a large apartment located in an exclusive quarter in the north of Tel Aviv. His children have the benefit of an expensive education.

Moral: do not lose hope even in the most desperate situations. You never know when the tide is going to turn.

□ *What is the next-best thing to settling down in Israel? To fall in love with a Tel Aviv Cinderella, marry her, and live in a genuine Israeli atmosphere — in New York.*

THE NOSE THAT ALMOST CHANGED THE COURSE OF HISTORY

———□———

MR. DAVID BEN-GURION
JERUSALEM

DEAR PREMIER,

Though I am only twenty-one, I have heard a great deal about your unsurpassed country. I am a great admirer of Israel. This I say not simply as a Jew, but also as an outspokenly intellectual type. I entertain particular respect for you personally, because of your outstanding achievements in the field of chemical research.

I have a small request of you. A few days ago, my relatives sent me a little box containing holy sand collected on the beach of Tel Aviv. We put it on the mantelpiece and everyone is admiring it. But that is not the point. The box was wrapped in an illustrated Israeli periodical named *Davar Hapoelet*. One picture showed a long line of young girls weeding the pampas or whatever you call it. My imagination was fired by the lithe figure of a teenage weeder, whose face was covered but whose charming nose stuck out of the line.

It was love at first sight. This girl embodies for me the Jewish people's rebirth from the agricultural point of view. I have to make her acquaintance or I don't know what I'm going to do. What a nose! My intentions are strictly honorable. Since I first saw her, I don't eat or drink, only walk in the clouds.

Enclosed is the photograph. Please find my bride. I am sure she is serving in the Army, probably as an officer.

Thank you in advance for the trouble you are taking in my behalf.

Yours sincerely, but really,
HARRY S. TREBITCH

TOP SECRET!
THE ISRAELI EMBASSY
PSYCHOPATHIC DEPARTMENT
WASHINGTON

WHO IS THIS CRACKPOT?

Hearty shaloms,
PRIME MINISTER'S OFFICE
DIRECTOR OF SEARCHES
TEDDY

PM OFFICE JERUSALEM
HIS DAD DONATED 200,000 TO UNITED JEWISH APPEAL STOP CAREFUL!

EMBASSY

MR. HARRY S. TREBITCH
NEW YORK

DEAR SIR,
You have again proved that Jewry's eternal light is still smoldering brightly. We hope to be successful in our search for the charming elected of your heart. A full-scale investigation has been started. The police are using bloodhounds especially trained for this kind of work.

THE SHORT STORIES OF EPHRAIM KISHON

As soon as we find the lady, we shall inform you by radio. Until then, I send you our best wishes.

Best regards to your dear daddy!
MINISTRY OF FOREIGN AFFAIRS
PHOTO IDENTIFICATION SECTION

YOUNG AMERICAN SEEKS HAPPINESS

"Either She — or No one!" Says The Wealthy Trebitch Scion — The Breathtakingly Beautiful Girl's Fatal Nose — The Young Couple Will Spend Their Honeymoon Together — The Century's Greatest Romance

(*By our Tel Aviv correspondent*) The whole country is following with bated breath the heart-warming romance of the young American millionaire and the bewitchingly charming Israeli shepherdess. The picture which fired young Trebitch's imagination is at present being scrutinized by the anthropological division of the Haifa Technion. Kol Yisrael is broadcasting every half hour the dramatic appeal of the police in which a money reward is offered to the finder. Visible peculiarity: a princely little nose turned upward at a 12-degree angle. During the past few days the Air Force has joined the search and its pursuit planes are combing the airspace on an around-the-clock basis. There is every hope that the two lovers will soon find each other.

STOP PRESS
The dawn identification parade at the Girl Tracing Center was unsuccessful. The fleet was mobilized.

MINISTRY OF FOREIGN AFFAIRS
PHOTO IDENTIFICATION SECTION
JERUSALEM

DEAR FRIENDS,
In reply to your letter we are sorry to inform you that we have not the faintest idea who the girls in the photo are. The only fact we succeeded

in ascertaining is that the issue in which the picture appeared was printed on August 3, 1937.

With best labor greetings,
THE EDITOR, *Davar Hapoelet*

STATE OF ISRAEL
MINISTRY OF FOREIGN AFFAIRS

MY DEAR HARRY S.,

Please forgive me for butting in on your most intimate personal affairs, but I feel that I have to express my admiration for your noble deed. Youthful love is a great thing, and love at first sight even more so.

At the same time, a sober thought comes to mind: would it not be wise to drop the whole matter? It was an unforgettably beautiful dream while it lasted, but perhaps it is better to forget it. Such things have happened before. You are still young, Harry S., you should travel, study, become world-wise, buy bonds. After all, a whole life of happiness is still before you.

Your true well-wisher,
GOLDA

FOREIGNGOLDA JERUSALEM
BOY GONE BERSERK STOP SEND NOSE OR NOT A RED PENNY TO YOU
FRANKLIN D. TREBITCH

MR. FRANKLIN D. TREBITCH
NEW YORK

DEAR SIR,

We have the pleasure of informing you that our border hunters have finally succeeded in locating the charming owner of the nose in question. The name of the happy creature is Fatma bint Mustafa El

Hadji. At our behest she divorced her husband, a resident of Abu Hirbat El Azun (Upper Galilee), and is already on the way to New York with the children.

Our sincere best wishes to the young couple. May the Lord give them much joy and happiness in this miserable life.

Your obedient servant,

TEDDY

ISREMBASSY WASHINGTON

HARRY S. TREBITCH VANISHED STOP LAST SEEN ALASKA

INTERPOL

□ *An uncle of mine, a politician by profession, once said to me: "Son, never join a ruling party which has only a nominal majority." That's why I became a writer. Indeed, the above axiom proves itself almost daily. In our parliament, which in Hebrew is called Knesset, the oppressed slaves of the ruling party do not dare to leave the meeting hall for any reason whatsoever lest they endanger the government majority in the next vote. That's what the poet meant when he wrote: "All hands are needed at harvest time."*

THE UNSUNG HERO

————□————

The following story is devoted to the unknown soldiers of Israel's democracy, to that handful of elected representatives who fulfill their duty to nation and party with a loyalty beyond the call of duty.

More specifically, this is the story of Knesset member I. L. Slutzkovski.

The time: two days before the Knesset vote on the controversial air pollution bill. In view of the bill's deep moral implications, it was decided for once to permit the MKs to cross party lines and to vote according to their consciences; that is to say, an agreement was concluded according to which in each party two members would be guided by their private consciences, and one would abstain. Furthermore, each side was apportioned an equal number of Arab MKs. And, last but not least, it was agreed between the government party and the Liberals that, for reasons of economy, each of them would leave one representative abroad: MK Dr. Bar-Bitzua, just then visiting his dentist in Stockholm, and the government emissary MK I. L. Slutzkovski, representing us at the Socialist Congress of the Headhunters of New Guinea.

The bomb exploded at the headquarters of the ruling party

exactly thirty-six hours before the fateful vote.

The big electronic brain at HQ which, coupled with long-range radar, tracks the 120 MKs twenty-four hours a day all over the globe, set off a warning buzzer on the master console. The blip on the map of Europe signaling Liberal Dr. Bar-Bitzua's whereabouts had suddenly started moving in a southerly direction. At daybreak the blip reached the border of the Fail-Safe Zone. The alert went out that as from that moment the hostile MK could make it to the ballot.

Five minutes later the complete emergency crew was chair-borne and direct contact was established with the High Command. The red phone jangled on the Prime Minister's desk.

"Dr. Bar-Bitzua landed in Rome at dawn," he was informed. "The Liberals have broken the agreement in order to win the vote. What shall we do?"

"Have Slutzkovski come at once!"

The cable from the Israeli Consul in Kokoda made it doubtful whether an adequate level of air pollution could be maintained in this country. I. L. Slutzkovski had set out for the Socialist Congress through the jungle, but in the meantime a typhoon had struck the island, making roads impassable to the extent that not even his salary could be sent after him, not to mention a message.

Every single operative at 110 Hayarkon realized what this meant: should the government fail to line up a majority, it would have to resign, anarchy would grip the country, tension would increase in the area, possibly a regional war, an inter-bloc clash, atoms, Armageddon.

The Operations Branch officers watched the Knessetoscope with growing alarm. The Bar-Bitzua blip was now nearing Cyprus, while that of I. L. Slutzkovski was still hovering futilely over the Sulawayo Range. Without further delay, an unequivocal order was flashed to the Kokoda consulate: "Find Parrot regardless of cost."

"Parrot" was Slutzkovski's code name in the operation. The Consul worked his connections with the aborigines and soon the big jungle drums were disturbing the island's quiet – two long throbs, three short thumps.... "White-tiger-who-always-tells-stale-jokes-return-at-once-to-King-for-show-of-hands. Over!"

Thus the urgent message of the Workers' Party of Israel was passed on from village to village. It reached Slutzkovski a day later on the banks of the Dorinoco.

"Bwana," the chief porter brought him the disconcerting news, "the tom-toms say Bwana has to go to 110 Hayarkon Street beyond the mountains or else."

"*Oy!*" Slutzkovski jumped up and rallied his men. "Get up, lazybones! We're returning to Kokoda!"

"Bwana, we won't budge from here," the head porter protested. "The jungle tribes are on the warpath."

"All right," I. L. Slutzkovski said, "then I'll return by myself!"

Slutzkovski set out in a dugout, but the primitive craft soon capsized and Parrot continued swimming. A posse of crocodiles trailed him for a while, but his awful swearing scared them off. He spent the night on the bank of the river, among the bamboo reeds. At about midnight a savage headhunter jumped on him from a coconut tree, but Slutzkovski produced his Knesset card and proved his immunity. On the way to the Dutch border post he was attacked by a black panther, but outran it. He reached the outpost at the end of his tether and collapsed.

"To Jerusalem," his parched lips whispered, "for the vote . . . ."

Jungle fever had completely sapped his strength and it looked as if he would never recover. International solidarity saved him. The Mayday message from the jungle outpost was monitored by a Siamese student, then transmitted by an Indian radio ham to a Serbian pharmacist, then to a Cypriot archbishop, and finally reached the Israeli Broadcasting Service, where it was mislaid. All this wireless traffic had wasted an awful lot of time, but it did not matter. Slutzkovski had in the meantime been flown to Bombay by American helicopter.

Tension in Hayarkon Street was well-nigh unbearable. It was decided that the Prime Minister should embark on a filibuster, so as to gain time. Who knows, maybe. . . .

At 8:30 in the morning the teleprinter started clacking: "Parrot's bus was involved in a fatal road accident on the border of Afghanistan. It caught fire and all passengers died, except for I. L. Slutzkovski, that dyed-in-the-wool party man. When last seen he was trying to get a ride to Iran."

To compound the disaster, it was discovered that M. Sulzbaum, MK – whose request for an appointment to the Finance Committee had been rejected – had vanished.

Two hours to the vote.

Slutzkovski reached the outskirts of Teheran completely worn out by the long walk. He found the Israeli Legation deserted, as all the officials were out searching for him. He phoned Hayarkon.

"Slutzki!" they shouted at the other end of the line. "They're voting in an hour's time. Fly here, for God's sake, fly!"

Taking advantage of the dawn mist, I. L. Slutzkovski slunk into the jetliner parked on the runway of Teheran Airport. He started the engines by intuition and took off into the rising sun. Two Iranian planes took off in pursuit, but collided at 8,000 feet. Over Upper Galilee the plane ran out of gas. Slutzkovski jumped out of it and got caught in the branches of a tree near Nazareth. A traffic cop freed him and gave him a ticket for jumping without a parachute.

The Prime Minister was not yet through with his marathon speech holding up the voting. He interspersed his remarks with amusing anecdotes and also gave a completely comprehensive historical review. The Opposition was becoming restive. Dr. Bar-Bitzua cut a pitiful figure on the Liberal benches, his swollen jaws proof of his aching teeth, his right arm secured by a rope the other end of which was held by the party whip. At the very last moment the Coalition had freed M. Sulzbaum from the washroom in which mysterious hands had locked him. But one vote was still missing. . . .

An urgent message reached the Prime Minister in the middle of his speech: "Slutzkovski's taxi was struck by lightning near Zichron."

The safety belt appeal contributed twenty precious minutes, but not more. The Opposition waived its right to reply. *The vote. . . .*

The Speaker is counting hands.

The Party Secretary, who has dragged Slutzkovski from Zichron by the scruff of his neck, is storming up the stairs.

Speaker: "The Opposition has fifty-six votes and one Member is asleep. The Government has fifty —"

Crash!

A mighty kick breaks down the door. Slutzkovski falls in, his arm raised.

"Fifty-seven votes for the Government," the Speaker intones. "The bill is defeated. Bye."

☐ *To prosper, industry needs an ample supply of organized, industrious and steadfast workers, a vast reservoir of skill and know-how. Of the above qualities, the "organization" angle is all right. Ours is a country of powerful trade unions. In line with this, every Hebrew industrialist knows that it is his duty to supply his workers at least once every two months with a reasonable pretext for striking. If he fails to cooperate in this field – strike!*

I'M ALL RIGHT, MOISHE!

———☐———

A lthough Israel Corks Ltd. was founded only a few years ago, it quickly became one of the most flourishing enterprises of our growing economy. It satisfied not only almost all the local demand for well-turned, high-quality corks, but even expanded into the Cyprus market and captured it. True, the plant enjoyed particularly sympathetic treatment at the hands of the authorities – that is, it received a 165-percent subsidy on each export dollar but there was nothing wrong with that, seeing that the raw material, high-grade oak cork, had to be brought in through Switzerland, and the workers through the Labor Federation. Economic circles considered Israel Corks Ltd. one of the country's most profitable companies, whose income would really start spiraling upward after our happily joining that unspeakable European Common Market.

The beginning of the labor crises can actually be pinpointed: September 27.

On that day Mr. Steiner, founder of the company and chairman of its board of directors, called in the head of the workers' council, one Joseph Ginzburg, and told him: "The plant is left all night long without supervision. It's a wonder no one has burgled it and carted everything away. This does not actually concern you, Ginzburg, but for the sake of good order I herewith inform you that the management has decided to hire a night watchman."

"But that definitely does concern me, Steiner," Joseph Ginzburg answered. "The workers' council has to approve the decision."

"I don't need any approval from you, Ginzburg," Mr. Steiner replied, "but all right."

As a matter of fact, the argument turned out to have been quite superfluous. The workers' council unanimously approved moving an elderly workman called Trebitch into the night watchman position on condition he be given certain benefits, such as a night allowance in view of the loneliness he was going to experience, and naturally a third of his salary income tax-free, never mind what they write in the books. The management accepted the conditions without protest and old Trebitch started his night beat. For a while all was smooth sailing, but after the first night's watch Trebitch went to his councilman and told him: "Ginzburg, I'm afraid all by myself."

The councilman informed the management of this new development. Mr. Steiner again gave proof of his anti-labor attitude and demanded that the old coward be returned to his former job.

Joseph Ginzburg cut the furious director down to size. "A human being is not a cork that you can toss about, Steiner," he told him. "We've already put a new worker into Trebitch's old job and we certainly won't let him be fired because of your lack of social feeling. For the sake of good labor relations I propose to put on a second watchman with the old man."

Steiner surrendered, as production costs for each two-centimeter cork ran to only 12 agorot and he was loath to interfere with the joy of production within the plant. On that night, therefore, two watchmen were sitting in the cramped room in which the actual cork production took place. But next morning old Trebitch walked up to Joseph Ginzburg and told him: "It's better now, Ginsburg, but we get terribly hungry at night. We need a buffet."

This time the clash between Mr. Steiner and the councilman took on epic proportions. The management would perhaps have agreed to hiring a woman to make hot soup for the two watchmen, but it rejected out of hand Ginzburg's demand that an electrician be employed to turn on the lights in the evening and turn them off at the crack of dawn.

"What next?" Mr. Steiner shouted. "Can't they turn off the lights themselves?"

"First of all, don't shout, Steiner, because I'm not impressed," Ginzburg remarked with his characteristic calm. "Secondly, of course they can handle the electricity – after all, they are not children, are they? However! However, turning off lights is certainly an additional duty which could take away another man's job. If the management wants to have the two watchmen do forced watches during the night, the council has no objections, but a watchman does not have to work as an electrician as well!"

Mr. Steiner blanched.

"Ginzburg," he whispered hoarsely, "that's exclusively the management's business!"

"Steiner," said the councilman, "let's ask the arbitration board."

As usual, they took out the collective contract and quoted sub-paragraph 27: ". . . the management may act independently regarding all technical arrangements within the plant, provided this does not change working conditions."

"Here you are," Joseph Ginzburg pointed out. "It changes them!"

"It does not change them!"

"It does!"

The argument raged for thirty-six hours before the Secretary of the local Workers' Council intervened and proposed a compromise which was also a face-saving device for the management of Israel Corks Ltd. It was agreed, in principle, that a woman would be hired to run the night buffet and a qualified electrician to handle the lighting; in fact, however, it would not be he who would turn the lights on and off, but the woman. The electrician would only supervise her from a technical point of view.

"It is my sincere hope," the Secretary declared at the signing of the minutes, "that this will end all misunderstanding in this important production branch, and that now all constructive forces will be devoted exclusively to the implementation of the new economic policy, the increase of production, the freezing of wages –"

"That will do," Ginzburg interrupted him. "No need to go into details."

Two whole days passed at the plant in an atmosphere of quiet, with no disturbances.

But on that Tuesday Mr. Steiner called in Councilman Ginzburg. The Chairman of the Board was sitting in his big armchair waving a sheet of paper in his hand.

"What's this?" Mr. Steiner hissed. "What on earth is this again?"

"An ultimatum," Ginzburg answered. "Why?"

The document in Mr. Steiner's shaking hand was a summary of the demands of the four night workers who had elected the veteran watchman Trebitch as their leader. It boiled down to the following points: (a) hiring a qualified porter to open and close the door for the night shift; (b) raising that part of the salary of which the income-tax authorities are ignorant, never mind the book juggling, by 15 percent, in view of the dry winter; (c) a young watchdog; (d) pensions; (e) an adequate number of mattresses and blankets.

The authors of the ultimatum called their demands a "minimum program" and hinted at severe disciplinary steps to be taken unless immediate negotiations were opened for the settlement of all differences.

"Ginzburg," Mr. Steiner gasped, his face livid, "I'll close down this damned factory, so help me!"

"That would be a lockout not approved by the Labor Federation and might prove rather dear," the councilman sneered, and added: "Who are you anyway, Steiner, to threaten us all the time?"

"I'm the owner of this firm! I'm its founder! I'm its director!"

"Look, I'm in no mood for your jokes, Steiner. The plant belongs to those who work in it."

"Who works here anyway? Making a cork costs us fifty-five agorot."

J.G. walked up and down for a while in a pensive mood, then drew up in front of the director.

"Steiner," he said sadly, "you're fired. Get your salary for last month and beat it."

A keen disappointment was in store for Joseph Ginzburg. The Union of Cork Workers within the Labor Federation did not approve of the dismissal.

"Comrade Ginzburg," they told the councilman at an informal meeting, "you can't fire a boss with fifteen years' seniority in the trade without paying him severance pay. Couldn't you give in on a few points in the ultimatum? For instance, why do you need a young watchdog?"

"You are lackeys of capitalism," Ginzburg dryly replied. "You are traitors to the working class and you are selling us down the river. But just think of the next elections, comrades!"

And he banged the door furiously behind him. The Trebitch group was by now in the third day of its slow-down strike. They came at night dragging their feet, the woman cooked the soup on a slow fire and they drank it with teaspoons. When connected labor branches joined them and bottle, brewery and nightclub workers staged one-and-a-half-minute warning strikes, the Central Committee of the Labor Federation saw itself forced to take emergency steps. They invited the capitalist to an informal meeting.

"Look here, Comrade Steiner," they explained to him, "this quarrel is over trifles, really. Why don't you want to increase a little that part of Comrade Trebitch's salary about which the comrades at the Income Tax know nothing? You can get mattresses, blankets, a porter and dogs from the development budget, and as for pensions, by the time those workers reach pensionable age, you'll long ago have lost control of the plant, so why worry?"

"It's a question of prestige," Comrade Steiner replied. "Rid me of this gang and I'll include you in my prayers."

"We shall agree to the cancellation of the night watch only if it can be proved beyond the shadow of a doubt that it has become superfluous. But for that the whole plant will obviously have to switch over to night work."

Thus Israel Corks Ltd. turned to producing corks at night, switching its full complement of employees to a single night shift which comprised six workers, the secretary and Mr. Steiner himself. At first certain difficulties arose over attendance at night school and cultural events, but with the help of certain technical improvements and a very long-term government loan, the management succeeded in fixing the price of the export corks at Sh.1 each. Tempers calmed down and production returned to normal.

Until one night, a few minutes after midnight, Mr. Steiner called into his office the head of the workers' council.

"The plant is completely unsupervised all day long," Mr. Steiner said. "Though this does not concern you, Ginzburg, for the sake of good order I hereby notify you that the management has decided to hire a watchman."

□ *Our thirst for culture cannot be stilled by the talent available at home, so we have to import some from abroad.*

A ROARING SUCCESS

———□———

One wet winter night, impresario N. N. Feinholz had a hot idea: why not bring to Israel the world's most famous lion tamers and give twenty-five gala shows at the Ramat Gan stadium?[1] Being a man of deeds, he flew to America, and soon had nine celebrities of the lion cage sign on the dotted line.

The impresario's calculation was as simple as it was realistic:

Airlifting 9 tamers and 83 lions to Tel Aviv (20 planes)	Sh. 54,000
Full board and lodging at the Accadia Hotel (25 days @ Sh.30,000)	750,000
Stadium rent for 25 nights	25,000
Unforeseen expenses	200
TOTAL	Sh.829,200

Now, the stadium has a capacity of 40,000 spectators. At Sh.5 a ticket, this spells an income of Sh.5 million, or a practically riskless profit of more than Sh.4 million (the income tax would be negligible).

The press published glowing reports of the spectacle, and especially of its star lion, named Beigele, which understood only

[1] It has become the rage with our large and not-so-large cities to build huge amphitheaters, a symptom for which a psychiatrist could no doubt easily find a suitable mental disorder. These arenas often have a capacity of 100,000, so that when there is a sellout, the rest of the country is practically deserted.

Yiddish. Newsreel photographers had a field day when the lions arrived at Lydda and were escorted by an armored column to the Accadia Hotel. A banquet[2] was given in the guests' honor, with the participation of the diplomatic corps, party leaders and sundry Cabinet Ministers. The lion tamers' spokesman, in an emotion-laden speech, disclosed that an old dream had come true with their arrival in India(!), as they had always wanted to go on a real tiger hunt. For the lions, the hotel kitchen cooked ten camels and thirty donkeys. All had a good time. A Ministry of the Interior department head toasted N. N. Feinholz and called him "the Churchill of the Middle East."

Two hundred glaring searchlights shone on the crowd of 20,000 at the premiere. According to the program, the mayor of Ramat Gan should have opened the show by entering the lion cage and cracking a gold-plated whip, but for some reason or other the mayor refused and cracked the whip outside the cage, hitting the Italian Ambassador's wife on the neck, so that she had to be treated at a nearby first-aid station.

After this brief incident, the big show started. Lions came, jumped through burning hoops, crouched on footstools, skipped ropes, and finally rose on their hind legs holding blue and white flags in their paws. (Stormy applause.) Then came the lions, and they jumped through hoops, crouched on footstools, did more rope skipping and waved more flags . . . then more lions . . . burning hoops . . . footstools . . . flag waving. . . .

The show lasted six and a half hours, but after four and a half the spectators were already showing signs of restlessness. Children started pelting the lions with pebbles.

The next evening a sharp decline in attendance made itself felt. As compared with the previous evening's 20,000, only 1,412 showed up on the second evening, 407 on the third, 18(!) on the fourth, and 7(!!) on the fifth (of these, 3 had complimentary tickets). The income no longer covered all the expenses.

[2] This again is a relic from Mandatory times. Although immune to cricket, we were badly stung by the banquet bug.

The impresario found himself in something of a predicament. By contract, there should have been twenty more shows, but he could no longer pay the lion tamers and the hotel bill. The tamers were also disappointed, because they had hoped to get rich in India, instead of which it transpired that they were in Israel.

The lion's alimentation deteriorated. On the sixth day they were served only six camels and nine donkeys, and after a week only six donkeys (for eighty-three lions!). The hungry beasts burst into frightful roars, disturbing the tourists at the hotel.

After ten days the Accadia Hotel management informed impresario Feinholz that if his bill was not settled within two days, the lions and their tamers would be evicted. In a huff, the impresario replied that he refused to have any truck with blackmailers, at which the management kicked the lions out of the hotel.

The lions split into small bands and showed up where they were least expected. When they ate Señor Alfonso Goldstein, chairman of the Uruguay United Jewish Appeal,[3] people were shocked and the press clamored for prompt police intervention. Police Headquarters washed its hands of the whole affair, saying it had no right to intervene in quarrels of a financial nature, and besides it lacked the funds for hunting lions. The Government Tourist Office considered organizing big-game hunts.

Following the impresario's disappearance, the authorities informed the Swiss Legation that they demanded the immediate evacuation of the lions at the Swiss government's expense, as they endangered the lives of Swiss nationals living in Israel. The Minister refused to oblige, pointing out the small number of persons involved. The authorities then appealed to the United States government for aid under its Point 4 program for technical assistance to underdeveloped nations.

The lions continued their irresponsible behavior. In Herzliya they

[3] The United Jewish Appeal is a world organization surpassed in its scope ony by the Vatican and Standard Oil. It collects $600 million a year from Jews who live abroad. The organization is extremely popular here in Israel.

devoured thirty-two passers-by within two days, and completely ruined that locality's reputation as a health resort. The lion tamers had banded together and busied themselves with highway and bank robberies. Twenty days later, rogue lions were sighted all over the country. One of them (as a matter of fact it was Beigele) blundered into the Histadrut building on Arlosoroff Street, and ate a clerk a day, without anybody missing them. His presence became known only after he ate the tea carrier. The army had to throw barbed-wire concertinas around government offices and party headquarters.

N. N. Feinholz, who at the time was basking in the Riviera sunshine, rang up the Finance Ministry and advised it to cover the lions' transportation expenses from a special tax on cigarettes.

But in the end, the problem was solved. The government succeeded in convincing UNESCO that the lions' evacuation would be in the spirit of international agreements for the prevention of genocide, after which a Swedish ship chartered by UNESCO removed twenty-one lions. (The lion's share of the lions had in the meantime starved or settled down to live off the land.) The five lion tamers who survived the pitched battle with the police protested against the hostile attitude of certain circles, but declared that the lions had nothing but praise for the taste of the Israeli public.

□ *Every nation has its hallmark. The Swiss save, the Germans eat, the Swedes drink, Englishmen strike, Japanese work, Spaniards bullfight, Indians multiply, Italians do nothing. The Jews envy.*

THE GREENING OF ISRAEL

Joseph the old elevator boy sat on a stool by his panel devotedly pushing the buttons while he read his morning paper. Between the fourth and fifth floor he gave us an accusing look and asked: "Read that? It says here that Israeli Textile Industries have exported $25 millions' worth of goods this year! I'm telling you, mister, the world ain't normal . . . ."

Joseph's face was a tormented green; his eyes were straight and narrow. He felt a fierce envy for Israeli Textile, seeing as how that miserable enterprise had managed to sell those miserable panties all over the world while he, Joseph, was stuck here at his buttons without any export opportunities.

Joseph's extremist view will surprise only those who keep no finger on our national pulse. We've been envious since the world began, right from the Day of Creation. Take Cain. When that lively lad saw how his brother was outdoing him at establishing connections Up There, he got mad and yelled: "Anything Abel can do, Cain can do Abler," and bumped off his brother in the field. He really started something, Cain did, a long and glorious Jewish history of unabated brother-envy. King Saul, for instance, was fit to kill when he saw how David could sing more prettily than he could, and King Solomon himself confessed: "Better a thousand women than one jealous wife."

Even our god is called a Jealous God, so what can you expect?

No doubt some honest citizens among us will argue the thing is universal, that men have always envied each other. We're not denying that envy is international, but the Chosen People choose their own way even in this.

In other countries, every horse-trader envies the next horse-trader, and every architect another architect, and every impresario is ready to roast his competitor over a slow flame. But traditional Israeli envy isn't classified by profession and social stratum, it spreads every which way. It's variegated, *comprehensive* envy. Stucks the plumber envies Shimon Perez. Shimon Perez envies Daniel Barenboim, and Barenboim envies the spy who came in from the cold. Israeli envy goes crosswise and spiralwise and in zigzags. Free-style, catch-as-catch-can envy.

The common Israeli citizen starts his day with a breakfast of sour grapes as he listens to the news. By the time he gets to his car, he's already green all over. When he pulls up before the forever amber lights he casts a hostile glance at the next-door driver, although he's never seen him before, and mutters to himself: "Who does he think he is, the sneak!" That's Preventive Envy, the you-never-know variety, based on the experience that you can always find some acceptable cause for the real thing, for Envy Proper.

And so we travel all day on the green wave, our jaundiced eye hunting for game, lips tight, tongue dry. Sometimes the various undercurrents combine into a huge flood of national envy, as in the case of Uri Geller, who unites the entire population from members of government to hewers of wood.

A few months ago, the Pathological Institute provided an accurate measuring unit for the common run of Israeli envy. It's called the "oi," one oi being the amount of envy needed to produce half a square inch of yellow foam about the envier's mouth, accompanied by audible teeth-gnashing. Following are the results of the Institute's research into the D.E.C. (Daily Envy Consumption) of the average citizen the world over:

Americans	17 oi
Japanese	3 oi
Spaniards	44 oi
Israelis	2,100 oi

(up to 3,000 in summer)

Not bad, what? Though as a matter of fact, the memorable Dayan Festival raised the national average considerably. The day he got divorced a wave of holy joy swept the country, strangers embraced in the street, lifelong enemies made it up — it was a positive enviers' reunion.

Then there's the dentist in Zichron Ya'acov who hated the Israeli movie star Topol (850 oi) from the bottom of his heart after he read in the papers of the star's triumphs in London. The irate doctor kept dreaming of *Fiddler on the Roof* getting bad reviews in TIME magazine, and then the miracle happened, the dream came true! The dentist bought up 150 copies of TIME and gave them away free to his patients, and ever since the man's changed out of all recognition. The glint is back in his eye, his sex life has improved, and he is taking a course in oil drilling.

The Israeli envier is always sending fervent prayers up to the Lord to ask for His personal intervention in tripping up the other fellow. This happens nowhere as often as in the theater. More than once the Lord God can be heard sighing to the cherubim: "They've two premieres in Israel tomorrow. Am I going to have a day!"

Like every national sport, envy calls for continual practice. The Israeli owes it to himself to keep an evergreen eye on the liquidity rates of the Mediterranean Envy Exchange. A new car, for instance, no longer raises excessive amounts of envy, only about 100 oi; a trip abroad still rates 250–300 oi. A personal appearance on TV and loud local publicity of whatever kind now stand at 500 oi. Enrichment from honest toil within the country creates roughly 3,600 oi (there's greater tolerance for enrichment at the public's expense: a bare 650 oi!). Any success abroad, on the other hand, may reach the staggering heights of 10,000–15,000 oi. The index for important invitations to high society has gone up steeply of late: dinner at the American Ambassador's produces 4,500 oi at present (an invitation from the Chief of Staff is 2,500). The invitation index is, of course, subject to the elementary Israeli rule that the invitation only takes full value if your fellow isn't invited.

The experienced envier is ever prepared with self-defense and counterattack. A few days back someone who shall be nameless asked us: "What, aren't you invited to cocktails with Rabin at five?"

"We couldn't have come anyway," we said. "At five we feed our dolphins."

The main thing is never to unbend for a moment, but to nurse one's stomach ulcers tirelessly in the spirit of the Eleventh Commandment: thou shalt begrudge! Daily envy is a duty in this country, it's a national asset, our children's future. What's more, it's a positive contribution to the country's development. Tiny Israel with its barren wastes and deserts will soon be covered with green.

☐ *In the beginning there was gasoline and the exhaust pipe, then were created the engine and the car, the horn and the traffic light. To these were added the parking meter, traffic signs and the traffic cop, and in the end Satan climbed out of the big city's sewer and changed Hell's name to "parking lot."*

What follows is a Biblical version of the story.

ONE HELL OF A JOB

─────────☐─────────

There was a man in the city of Tel Aviv whose name was Job Kunstatter; and that man was perfect and upright, and one that feared the law, and eschewed evil.

And there were born unto him seven sons, and he had a pickup truck.

And that man was the most virtuous of his generation, and he drove most cautiously on the roads and highways, and he went to and fro in the country and walked up and down in it, and never once was he laid hand on by traffic cops and given a ticket. Also Job paid his municipal taxes before they were due, and furthermore he was alone in his generation who did thus.

Now there came a day when the sons of the Municipality came to present themselves before the Mayor, and Satan came also among them.

And the Mayor said unto Satan, "Hast thou considered my servant Kunstatter? There is none like him in the city, a perfect and an upright man, one that feareth the laws and escheweth evil."

Then Satan answered the Mayor and said, "Hast thou not made a hedge about him all his life? But put forth thine hand now and take all that he hath, and he will curse thee to thy face."

And Satan and the Mayor then and there made a wager. And the

Mayor said unto Satan, "Behold, all that he hath is in thy power; only upon himself put not forth thine hand." So Satan went forth from the presence of the Mayor and that is how it all started.

It came to pass one morning that Job Kunstatter rose from his bed and went down into his yard and black darkness fell on his eyes and he staggered. That is because he always parked his truck in the yard at night, as it was difficult to find parking space in the busy street. But on that morning a behemoth of a truck stood in the gate of the yard and blocked the way to him. Job shouted and honked and also went and asked the neighbors about the owner of the truck, but he found not his identity until 10:30 A.M., when the man came with measured steps and it was Eliphaz the Parker.

"Man," Job lifted up a cry. "Dost thou not see that this is a gate to the yard?"

"I see nothing," quoth the truck driver. "I make parking where I want."

And he went forth and parked likewise on the morrow and on Thursday. Job's eyes knew no sleep at night from fear that he might arise in the morning and find the exit blocked before his pickup truck, for only with it could he earn his bread. Then he got up at dead of night and went down in the street to look and even put slips of paper on the truck of Eliphaz the Parker which read, "I warn thee for the last time, thou swine, that thou shalt stop parking in front of the gate." Nor did this help at all, for Eliphaz was much bigger than he and his body had waxed fat on him.

Job became a nervous wreck, but in all this he sinned not, nor charged the Mayor foolishly. He went to the police and lodged a complaint against Eliphaz the Parker.

"We cannot do anything," the police told him, "as long as there are no official signs before the entrance to thy yard."

"If so," quoth Job, "I shall observe the words of the Prophet."

For thus said Jeremiah, "Set up signs," and Job did not spare time and effort to attain his goal. He hurried to the Road Marking Department of the Municipality and submitted an application which was rejected out of hand and Job submitted an appeal and again pleaded and was again sent packing and came back and would not give up.

"Shall we receive good at the hand of the authorities and shall we not receive evil?" he asked and did not rest, until one day two inspectors rolled into his courtyard and found that the place was pleasant in their eyes for parking purposes and approved his application, and barely two years later two proud signs were standing at the two sides of the entrance: "Five yards. Entrance to courtyard," and on the other side, "End of restriction."

And there was great rejoicing and his sons made a feast unto their friends and were merry with wine all night and Kunstatter rose very early and went out into the courtyard and black darkness fell on his eyes, for the gate was again blocked to the pickup truck. A great shout arose from Job's mouth and he ran straight to the cop on his beat.

"I know, sir, I know," the cop calmed him. "I have already written out a ticket for the offender."

That is to say, cars had multiplied so bountifully in the crowded city that the citizens had no choice but to park on every empty space, even at the risk of a 10-shekel fine for not obeying the signs.

"It's worth every shekel," Eliphaz the Parker informed Job. "Although it costs me a few shekels every moon, I have not to search for a parking space in the dust."

And not only he but others also parked in front of the courtyard between the signs and Job rent his mantle and shaved his head and fell down upon the ground and worshipped.

"The righteous suffer," he shouted, "and the wicked rejoice."

Then a cloud of dust fell on the courtyard and Job's wife stepped out of it.

"Why dost thou lie there and weep?" the woman asked. "I shall tell thee what thou must do. Simply put thine own pickup between the signs at night and no one else shall take away thy place."

And Job did as he was told, and after many moons of heartbreak and nights of unrest, sleep again returned to his eyes. And the man rose early with joy in his heart and went down into his courtyard and black darkness fell on his eyes because on the windshield of his pickup truck was glued a life-size ticket.

Job ran to the cop on his beat and foamed, "Why didst thou write me a ticket, O cop?"

The cop pointed at the signs.

"What is written there, sir? 'No Parking,' yes?"

Job sounded his famous laughter. "Ha ha. They set up those signs for me, that I may come out of my courtyard with my pickup in the morning."

"Go out then, sir," said the cop, "but stand not thy car where parking is forbidden!"

"But is it forbidden for me?"

"Of course for thee and for everybody else too, sir.'

"Dost thou not understand? This is *my* sign."

"Then thou must serve as an example to others, sir."

And on the morrow there was again a ticket on the windshield, and Job sprinkled dust upon his head and shouted, "Why have signs if there be no redemption in them? If I park in the courtyard, they block me. If I park outside, they ticket me. Let the day perish wherein I was born."

In those days Job Kunstatter no longer did anything but deal with sign matters, and his face dropped and his steps faltered. He spent half his life between the walls of the various departments trying to have justice done.

"The police must impose fines according to regulations," they explained to him. "It is not written on the signs that the place belongs to thee."

But Job answered and said, "If so, write it there!"

"Oh, no," the authorities said. "Only diplomats and well-known politicians are entitled to reserved parking places in the street. An ordinary mortal like thee can get at best free entrance to his courtyard. By the way, why dost thou park outside when there is room in thy courtyard?"

After this, Job opened his mouth and cursed all those present and he was kicked out and marked a callous wrongdoer and his fingerprints were taken. And he removed the tickets every morning and did not pay a penny and was hauled into court and found guilty and his calamity was very great and his family was troubled lest one night he die. And one morning he went down into the street and lo and behold! there was no trace of his pickup truck between the signs, because the patience of the police had run out and they had towed it away to a safe place so that it should not obstruct the entrance to the yard.

Thereupon Kunstatter's nerves snapped and he said, "Is my strength the strength of stones? Or is my flesh of brass? Until when will I be afflicted by traffic cops?"

His sons became fed up and scattered unto the four corners of the world and his wife packed her bags.

"Dost thou still retain thine integrity?" his wife said unto him. "Dost thou not see that the signs are ruining thee? Have them removed and thou wilt be able to park in front of thy house without being fined."

Then Job hurried to the Municipality and fell down in the dust before the Traffic Commission and beseeched it to remove from his head the visitation of the signs.

"And what dost thou think this is – the marketplace or the palace of authority?" the officials flared. "Only yesterday or the day before thou pressed us relentlessly to install signs in front of thy yard."

"That was long ago," Job answered. "Hidden are the ways of traffic in our city, amen."

The authorities dropped a sympathetic tear.

"The heart weeps for thee but our hands are tied," they said. "Because it is not thou that wast given the signs but the parking place in thy yard, and as long as the yard stands, there must be free access to it."

"I shall go forth," Job stuttered, "and destroy the yard. I shall blow it up. I shall scatter antitank obstacles all over it."

He was kicked out bodily from all commissions and did not know rest to the end of his days.

As a matter of fact Satan, whose idea, it will be remembered, the little game had been, had long ago won his wager and things simply rolled on by themselves. One moonless night the cop on his beat noticed a dark figure using a big saw on a street sign, and before Job could complete his task he was arrested by the cop and hauled before the judge. For five months Kunstatter sat in a dark hole of a prison and the curses never ceased flowing from his mouth, so much so that his jailers stopped their ears with moss.

It is said that on his release Job found that his pickup truck had been stolen, but not even this redeeming news could cure his sick spirits, and his tracks vanished into the wilderness. According to legend he still wanders around in the southern desert, and tourists relate that sometimes his eerie laughter is to be heard in the distance and he is seen running along the skyline sounding a car horn 140 times.

☐ *Our sweet native-born kids, apples of our eye, are six feet two inches in the shade and their attitude to their fathers is definitely parental. In our schools, corporal punishment has been introduced long ago. Otherwise how could one cope with the teachers?* ·

GOODBYE, MR. CHIPS

SEPTEMBER 13. Today I started my pedagogical career at an elementary school, where I am replacing a fugitive teacher. Wonderful feeling, to have a roomful of sweet and lively sabras¹ hanging on your every word.

The first lesson began most auspiciously. But somewhat later – after about a minute, that is – a pupil in the first row called Zatopek turned on his transistor. I warned him three times that I wouldn't tolerate light music in class. In the end I lost my temper and ordered him out.

"You get out!" Zatopek replied and went on fiddling with the knobs in search of pop music on short-wave. I hurried down to the headmaster. He warned me that under no circumstances ought I to leave the classroom. "If one of you has to get out, it certainly must be him!" the headmaster stated. "Never show signs of weakness!" I returned to class and demonstratively lectured on the Song of Deborah. But I am sure that Zatopek nurses a grudge against me.

SEPTEMBER 27. There has been a rather unpleasant incident. We don't yet know for certain who is to blame. As far as I can remember, the scuffle started after I spotted a spelling error in Zatopek's essay. In the sentence "We are crazy about Bible studies" the boy had

---

¹ It is said that the American faster-than-sound Saber jets were named after our sweet-and-livelies. Paradoxically these youngsters were born to meek Jewish mothers and fathers.

misspelled the first word as "Ve." I stood behind Zatopek while he was writing and pointed out this serious error to him. Thereupon he seized a ruler and hit me across the fingers. It hurt! I am not a champion of blind discipline in our educational system, and I reject corporal punishment as a pedagogical tool. I immediately asked the errant student to send me his parents, and complained to the headmaster.

"According to Ottoman Law, a pupil may hit his teacher, but the teacher may not hit back," the headmaster explained. "Don't get too near to them."

SEPTEMBER 28. This morning Zatopek's parents dropped in, the mother, two fathers and a number of uncles. "So my boy is an idiot?" one of the fathers roared. "My boy can't write, hey?" There followed a brief but stormy exchange of blows and then they tried to push me against the wall, but I was not impressed and nimbly slipped between their legs and locked myself in the headmaster's room. The parents battered on the door.

"They'll break it down in a minute," the frightened headmaster whispered. "Better surrender."

I explained to him that this would irretrievably tarnish my father image in the students' eyes. The boys dragged some benches into the corridor and lined up along the wall to have a better view, cheering on the Zatopeks.

Luckily, an inspector of the Ministry of Education arrived and enforced a truce. According to the compromise agreed on through his mediation, Zatopek's parents evacuated the building, and ve shall no longer meddle with the students' spelling.

OCTOBER 9. Today's demonstrations were particularly rowdy. About a dozen senior students milled about the barbed wire fence thrown up around the school building, and somewhat later burned me in effigy. I realized that matters had got out of hand and went to consult the headmaster.

"You see, these are the ways of our fighting, pioneering youth," the veteran pedagogue explained. "They were born in a free country. They are sons of the desert. They utterly lack inferiority complexes.

You cannot get through to them with conventional scolding and punishments. They appreciate only bullies of Matuska's sort."

Matuska is our PT teacher, a pleasant fellow weighing two hundred pounds. Strangely enough, at his lessons complete silence and order reign, and it seems that the pupils' parents do not bother him with complaints. I asked the headmaster what Matuska's secret was.

"He's simply a pedagogue," the headmaster said. "He never touches his pupils. He only kicks them."

I started taking judo lessons at a gymnasium. In my group of twelve, all were teachers. I made up my mind to hit back. The headmaster does not yet know about this.

OCTOBER 21. Our trade union informed us that the Minister of Finance was dead set against special "danger pay" for teachers because, in his view, so far there has been no open fighting on the educational front. That's a pity. I owe money to everybody: the grocer, the insurance man and also the lawyer who is drawing up my will. Because I have decided to fail Zatopek in grammer.

Half my fortune, Sh.25 in cash, I willed to the hostel for paralyzed teachers and to widows whose husbands fell on the field of education in the line of duty. I informed the headmaster that yesterday they had shot at me from a rooftop. He advised me to stay indoors until after the exams.

Anyway, I failed Zatopek.

OCTOBER 22. I had clean forgotten that Zatopek's brother was a sergeant major in the Artillery. The bombardment started in the morning while we were discussing Herzl's vision. We hurried down into the shelter built a few years ago after the son of an Air Force pilot had flunked his math course. About twenty shells exploded nearby.

Around noon the director went out with a white flag and brought back the rebels' terms:

" 'Fair' in grammar and an apology."

Only the right wing of the school was damaged.

The students were not satisfied with my apologies (which they said were not sincere) and took the headmaster as a hostage. I phoned the Minister of Education and protested against the humiliations we teachers have to endure. How can we serve as a model to our pupils if we must always walk in pairs lest they jump us from behind? It is a question of professional dignity. A headmaster who is slapped every day loses face. The Minister promised to look into the matter, but at the same time warned us against further blackmail.

NOVEMBER 15. What I have dreaded all the time has happened. Zatopek caught a cold. This morning a posse of policemen came to the school and arrested me, as the boy had denounced me for criminal negligence. In vain did I assure them that it was not I who had left the window open. Zatopek's family unanimously testified against me. The representative of the Red Cross asked whether I had any request before the trial.

I mused as I was lying on my cot. "The solution to Israel's educational problems," I muttered, "is remote control . . . the teacher must be removed as far as possible from his pupils . . . far, far, way up there, like a highest authority, a sort of god . . . but how . . . ?

NOVEMBER 16. A miracle has happened. I opened the newspaper and . . .

We are no longer in danger of our lives.

Educational TV is on its way.

In the nick of time.

□ Every schoolboy knows that the Middle East is a hotbed of genuine hospitality. It is said that noble Bedouin sheikhs may have you a whole year in their tent without giving you even the slightest hint that perhaps it is time to beat it. Unfortunately, the number of noble Bedouin sheikhs among Tel Aviv waiters is strictly limited.

CLOSING TIME

———□———

The time was 11:30 P.M. and we did not yet feel like hitting the sack. We had just seen a very vulgar show and were itching to start the post-mortem. We walked a few steps up moonlit Dizengoff Street and decided to end the pleasant evening in an appropriate way.

"Come," the wife proposed, "let's have a glass of tea."

We entered the first restaurant we came across. It was a small but intimate spot, with colored fluorescent lights, a shining espresso machine and two undressing waiters. The only other person present was a bald man who wiped the bar counter with a dirty rag. As we came in, he looked at his watch and said something to one of the waiters, who thereupon slipped again into his time-worn white jacket. The air was fraught with social ferment, but we ignored and resolutely sat down at one of the tables.

"Tea," I sang out. "Two teas!"

The waiter appeared to hesitate for a few seconds, then stepped into the kitchen. We heard him ask behind the door, his voice filled with hatred: "Any boiling water left?" Meanwhile the waiter had started folding the tables outside. He did this with clipped movements and staccato noises, as if underscoring the ruthless flight of time. The first waiter came running with two glasses of tea and plunked them down on our table, an irritated expression on his face. We stirred the tea for a while, hoping to warm it up a degree or two, then started discussing the vulgar show.

"Pardon me . . .".

It was Baldhead. He lifted our glasses and removed the much-spotted cover from the table. We did not mind, because the rough-grained, coffee-etched tabletop looked quite pleasant to the eye, but in the meantime the first waiter had taken off his white coat and was now standing in a blue raincoat at the doorway, waiting. The second waiter finished the folding and turned off the neon sign outside.

A certain uneasiness gripped us.

"Could it be," I whispered to the little one, "could it be that they want us to go?"

"Maybe," the wife replied. "Don't look!"

The tension rose by leaps and bounds. Obviously, any sign of weakness would have been fatal in this situation, so we went on whispering excitedly at our isolated table. Soon afterward the raincoated waiter sidled up and held a plate with the bill under my nose. I pushed the piece of chinaware aside and Raincoat retreated. Baldhead took the little one's hat off the rack and delicately placed it on our table.

"Thank you," the little one said to him. "Have you got cakes?"

Baldhead shuddered and looked backward at the second waiter, who was combing his hair in front of the mirror. The silence lasted for what seemed an eternity, but in the end one of the waiters, the raincoated one, threw down in front of us a nondescript cheesy something. The little one dropped her fork and a new one had to be fetched. If looks could kill. . . .

"I can't hold out much longer."

"You must!"

The lights in the restaurant went off and on several times, but we took this, too, in our stride. Baldhead rang down an iron shutter with an ear-shattering bang, then locked the courtyard door, turning the key twice with ominous finality. A grimy old crone slouched in from the kitchen carrying bucket and ragmop and started scrubbing the floor.

"Watch out, ma'am."

With that the old lady pushed the ragmop under our table. We raised our legs high so as to afford her access. The well-combed waiter in the meantime walked through the restaurant, lifted the chairs and placed them upside down atop the tables. By then we felt clearly that we were *personae non gratae*.

"But," I whispered to the little one, "why don't they tell us to go?"

"It embarrasses them," the wife informed me, "they are trying to be polite."

Through half-lowered eyelids I surveyed the scene. The first waiter was standing out in the street, watching us. The other waiter had just about finished upturning the chairs. Baldhead put on a black beret and opened a small cupboard on the wall. The lights went out in a flash and only a little moonlight filtered in through the door. Then I felt someone placing a chair on my back. I groped in the darkness for the wife's hand. Those were climactic moments.

"I say," I heard the wife's voice, "have you got magazines?"

That was the proverbial last straw. For a brief while one could feel the air quivering, then Baldhead struck a match and came over to us from the door.

"Excuse me," he said, and his face was flushed in the flickering light, "we close at midnight."

"Then why didn't you say so?" I asked. "How could we have guessed?"

We brushed the chairs off our backs, paid and left, skidding on the wet floor tiles. The time was 11:48, Eastern Mediterranean Time.

THE NEANDERTHAL
SWEEPSTAKES

———□———

APRIL 7. Today our table collapsed under the weight of the festive dinner. My wife did not mind this in the least, because for quite a while she had wanted to get rid of the doddering piece of furniture. I sawed it into pieces and made a bonfire with them. The wife says that in Jaffa you can buy tables straight from the manufacturer. Cheaper, quicker. Tomorrow we are going to Jaffa.

APRIL 8. We place our order with a carpenter named Joseph Neanderthal, whom we found to be possessed of a personality more winning than that of his competitors. He was up to his ears in work, sawing up huge planks lengthwise, his powerful chest framed by a clean undershirt, giant machines roaring all around him. He asked for Sh. 360 for the table, half of it in advance. The little woman tried to bargain with him, but he cut her short.

"Ma'am," Joseph Neanderthal said, looking straight into her eyes, "Neanderthal gives you responsible work. That's the price, not a cent less!"

He made an excellent impression on us. "That's the way an honest man talks," my wife whispered. I asked when the table would be ready. Neanderthal took out a little notebook from his pocket. Monday at noon. My wife told him we were eating standing up, etc. Neanderthal went to consult his partner, came back and said Sunday evening, and that was that. We would have to pay the delivery man. I paid half in advance and we left. Neanderthal shook our hands and looked straight into our eyes, as if he were saying, "You can trust me!"

APRIL 14. Last night we waited for the table. It did not arrive. This morning I rang up Neanderthal. The partner told me that right now Neanderthal was not in and he himself did not know a thing about any table. As soon as Neanderthal came in, he would ring us. He did not ring us. Embarrassing. We are eating, I am ashamed to confess, on the carpet.

APRIL 15. I rode down to Jaffa to kick up a storm. Neanderthal was up to his ears in work. Under his powerful hands a circular saw was spurting jets of sawdust. I had to introduce myself because he did not remember me. Then he explained that there had been a little hitch. His worker had been called up for army reserve duty. He promised 4 A.M. day after tomorrow. In the end we settled for 3:30. I had stipulated three o'clock, but he could not make it. "Neanderthal is like a precision watch," he said. "He never makes empty promises.

APRIL 17. Nothing. I rang up. The partner told us that Neanderthal had cut his left hand, so the table would not be ready until tomorrow. Another day really does not count.

APRIL 18. The delivery man did not come. My wife says she had known right from the beginning this would happen. She had found the crook's very looks untrustworthy. The woman called Jaffa. Neanderthal answered the call. He spoke soothing words. The wood had developed tension, but he had put it in a press frame and now the table was practically ready. What does it look like, the wife wanted to know. "The legs are not yet in position," stated Neanderthal. "In three days' time it will be ready for delivery (the polishing itself should take two days)." All right. We take our meals sitting cross-legged on the floor. It is not too difficult – simply a matter of practice.

APRIL 21. The partner rang us up on his own initiative. The polisher is down with mumps. My wife got hysterics. "Ma'am," the partner said, "we could have finished the table in a jiffy. But we want to give you first-class workmanship. Tomorrow at two o'clock you'll have your furniture and we'll empty a bottle of beer."

APRIL 22. They did not bring it. I rang up. Neanderthal came to the phone. He does not know a thing. Promised his partner would call us.

APRIL 23. I took the bus to Jaffa. Neanderthal was up to his ears in work. When he noticed me, he started shouting would I please stop bothering him all the time, he could not possibly work under such pressure. The table is in the works, he informed me in a calmer mood, and took me to the storage shed where he showed me the planks. A special wood. Steel-hard. When? At the end of next week. Sunday at 10 A.M. he will call me. That's only fair, isn't it?

MAY 5. This morning my wife said to me, "It won't be ready." I said, "I have a feeling that this time it will be ready." "You'll see," said the little one. "His saw will break." I rang him up at noon. Neanderthal answered. They are still working on the table. There are certain difficulties with the formica. He does not want to give me a second-rate material. So the little one was wrong after all. The saw did not break; it is the formica. By the end of next week.

MAY 12. It did not arrive. According to my wife it will be ready maybe in a month's time. I say a fortnight, at the outside. I rang up. The partner came. Neanderthal has been away since the day before yesterday. He is seeing about the customs duty. But if memory serves him, Neanderthal had said something about the table being ready in three weeks' time. There is no need to call any more. On June 3, in the morning, the delivery man will show up with the furniture. I said to the woman, "You said a month, I a fortnight. It's going to be three weeks, so it's a draw." We are eating Roman-style – reclining. It is fairly comfortable.

JUNE 3. Nothing. I gave him a call – no answer. My wife – the middle of August. I – end of July. I went to Jaffa. At the bus stop, a taxi pulled up, the driver stuck out his head and hollered, "Neanderthal, Neanderthal!" Two other passengers got in. One of them has been on duty for the past six months in the matter of a footstool; the other, a teacher of physics, for only two months. We became friendly on the way there. Only the partner was in. Everything will be all right, he promised, and not only that, he whispered in my ear, but Neanderthal had specifically said the end of July, one hundred percent. I peeped into the storage shed; the steel planks were gone.

On the way back we discussed Neanderthal's personality. In what sort of work is he immersed all the time? Why does he behave the way he does? After all, this is killing him too. He looks like a hunted animal.

We decided to meet again next week at the Neanderthal line terminus.

My wife denies she ever made a bet for the end of August. I said, angry, "All right, from now on we are putting it down in writing."

JULY 30. I bet Sh.5 on the Feast of Tabernacles. The woman wagered on the end of the Gregorian year. Presumed excuse for the delay – a son will be born to Neanderthal. I – a short circuit. We duly recorded the bets.

Another Neanderthal fan joined us at the terminus, an elderly Supreme Court judge (cupboard – two years). The convoy set out for Jaffa. Neanderthal was up to his ears in work. He shouted that he could not possibly talk to each one of us separately. They appointed me their spokesman. Neanderthal promised, this time solemnly, the end of November. My table even earlier, around the Jewish New Year. Why so late? He is going to have a baby daughter. On the way back I told my partners about the bet with my wife. The teacher proposed we should bet among ourselves as well. On Maze Street there is a printer (armchair); he could print us betting forms. We decided to set up an exclusive club.

AUGUST 21. This time the meeting took place in our apartment. Thirty-one participants. The judge put the finishing touches to the Neanderthal Club statutes. Full-fledged members only from six months upward. Other clients could be only candidate-members. We checked the items on the betting form: (a) Promised date; (b) Excuse; (c) When will it be ready? (day, month, year.) We decided to commission an oil painting of Joseph Neanderthal, up to his ears in work, looking straight into your eyes. The members of the club are extremely nice people, all of them, without exception. We are one big, happy family. All of us are eating on the floor.

JANUARY 2. Today it was my turn to call on Neanderthal. He apologized for the delay. He had to appear in court, and that caused a certain loss of time. He pulled out a little notebook from his pocket, looked into it and said that tomorrow afternoon he would start working on my table. At home we filled out the forms. My wife – June 1. I – January 7, next year.

FEBRUARY 1. Gala meeting of the club. The membership is increasing by leaps and bounds: one hundred and four persons are participating in the sweepstakes. A beautician bet Sh.50 on her chest of drawers (January 15: "flu with kidney complications" – July 7) and won Sh.500 by guessing correctly the first two items, the promised date and the excuse. The gala meeting opened with chamber music performed by our quartet (three chairs and a Venetian blind). Then – within the framework of our cultural program – a professor lectured on the subject "The Table: a Superfluous Piece of Furniture." He set out to prove that Neanderthal man had eaten crouching on the ground and that this was very healthy. After the banquet we set out in three buses for a mass pilgrimage to Jaffa. Neanderthal was up to his ears in work. He promised to finish everything by 2 P.M. next Friday. The delay was due to a death in the family.

SEPTEMBER 4. Our Executive Committee decided today to set up a medical aid society for our members and to call it the Joseph Neanderthal's Clients' Sick Fund. It was also decided to publish a monthly magazine entitled *Eternity*, which would deal with current problems – descriptions of new machinery in Neanderthal's workshop, lists of workers on military reserve duty, results of the expanded betting pool, conducted tours through Old Jaffa, what's new in carpentry, etc. The training of our basketball team is proceeding nicely. We also discussed the possibility of raising capital for the construction of a clubhouse. At the end of the meeting, as prescribed by the statutes, we rang Jaffa. Only the partner was in; Neanderthal has gone on honeymoon. The partner promised to expedite matters. My wife placed Sh.300 on August 17, three years from now.

JANUARY 10. Something inexplicable has happened. In the morning, Joseph Neanderthal showed up in our doorway dragging some sort of table. We wondered what on earth he was up to. Neanderthal reminded us that once upon a time we had ordered this piece of furniture from him and here it was now. Clearly, he had gone out of his mind. His eyes were burning with a mad flame. "Neanderthal promises, Neanderthal delivers," he said. "Kindly pay the delivery man."

It was a horrible blow. Goodbye club, goodbye meetings, tours, exciting sweepstakes. All went down the river. And to top it all, we simply don't know what to do with the table. We can no longer eat sitting. The wife proposes to lie down under it at mealtimes.

This little drama with the Shakespearean title strives to describe a very special situation indeed: the Hebrew plumber has come by mistake and in a moment of complete abandon has repaired the dripping faucet. Now the time has come to pay him his well-earned wages. In this context the kind reader should remember the Chinese hangman's favorite torture, in which water drips at a measured beat on the victim's skull.

AS MUCH AS YOU LIKE

———————□———————

CAST: *Kishon, Mrs. Kishon, Stucks*

STUCKS (*Walks up slowly and stops in front of Mr. Kishon, who is reading his paper. Clears his throat.*): Well, Mr. Kishon, I fixed that bathroom tap. It wasn't an easy job, so help me, but that tap won't drip again, Mr. Kishon, I'm telling you, Mr. Kishon. I had to file down the cylinder a little bit, but I won't charge you for the filing, Mr. Kishon. I put in two new washers, they'll hold the water as it's never been held before . . . .

KISHON (*Goes on reading his paper.*)

STUCKS (*Drops his tool kit with an ear-splitting crash.*): So, as I said, I finished the job, Mr. Kishon, I finished it completely. (*Silence.*) I absolutely finished. I finished the job, damn it. Are you deaf?

KISHON: What? Oh, thank you very much, old boy. All right, goodbye.

STUCKS: I said, I finished with that tap!

KISHON: Well, about time, too!

STUCKS: Why "about time, too?"

KISHON: Look here, old boy, you had me come to your place for a whole month before you did me the honor of repairing that blasted tap.

STUCKS: That's because I'm so busy, Mr. Kishon. I'm always in a hurry. I'm always on the run. I haven't got a minute. What minute? Half a minute I haven't got. And why is that tap blasted?

KISHON: All right, so it isn't blasted.

STUCKS: Then why did you call it blasted?

KISHON: All right, I'll apologize to the tap. All right?

STUCKS: One has to watch one's language, Mr. Kishon. One never knows when and where!

KISHON: That will do, old boy. How much do I owe you?

STUCKS: (*Takes out paper and pencil.*): Well, let's see . . . I put in two new washers . . . I won't charge you for the filing . . . . (*Pulls out big watch from his pocket and looks at it.*) It's now six-thirty. Let's see. That tap is going to hold the water, Mr. Kishon. You don't have to worry. So maybe pay me, Mr. Kishon, let's say – as much as you like.

KISHON: Just tell me your price, old boy, we won't quarrel over it, right? (*Slaps his back.*)

STUCKS: Right. (*Suddenly he slaps Kishon's back.*) Because I fixed that tap, you know, I fixed it beautifully. It's going to last, Mr. Kishon, as long as you live.

KISHON: Splendid.

STUCKS: It may even last five years!

KISHON: Fine. But now, really, how much do I owe you?

STUCKS: Right. Now I really got to tell you. It's getting late. So, Mr. Kishon, if you too think that I fixed it properly, pay me – as much as you like.

KISHON: Now this I don't like. What do you mean, "as much as you like?" I have no time for making calculations. You fixed the tap nicely and you'll just as nicely tell me what you charge. So much and so much . . . .

STUCKS: How much?

KISHON: So much and so much and so much. That's how civilized people do business, right?

STUCKS: Right. You are absolutely right. That's how civilized people do business.

KISHON: But this is ridiculous, so help me! Tell me, old boy, how much do you usually charge for fixing such a small tap?

STUCKS: It wasn't such a small tap.

KISHON: All right. For such a big tap.

STUCKS: It wasn't so big either. (*Shows size of tap on palm of his hand.*) It was about this big. A medium-sized tap, two inches . . . .

KISHON: So for a two-inch tap.

STUCKS: More than two inches.

KISHON: For a tap more than two inches big.

STUCKS: It could have been even three inches. I couldn't swear to it. Let me check. Just a second! (*Prepares to return to bathroom.*)

KISHON (*Stops him.*): For all I care, it could be a thousand inches big, boy.

STUCKS: No, Mr. Kishon, it certainly wasn't a thousand inches big. There is no such thing. I'm almost sure that tap was between two and three inches big.

KISHON: All right, so how much do you charge for fixing a tap between two and three inches big?

STUCKS: You mean the repair, Mr. Kishon?

KISHON: That's right.

STUCKS: It must have been three inches after all. Now I'm sure.

KISHON: For goodness' sake, how much do you charge?

STUCKS: That differs from case to case, Mr. Kishon. Some people appreciate honest work. Others – quite to the contrary, Mr. Kishon – are stinking misers, dirty swine, miserable –

KISHON: How much does someone pay who isn't such a swine?

STUCKS: Such a person is not just a swine, Mr. Kishon, but also a stinking miser, a dirty swine, a miserable crook, that's what such a person is.

KISHON: How much does a person pay who is not a stingy swine, a dirty crook, a miserable, despicable, depraved miser, how much does he pay?

STUCKS: He always pays more.

KISHON: But in terms of money?

STUCKS: Of course in terms of money. I don't take checks.

KISHON: Listen, old boy, if you think you'll succeed in driving me out of my mind, you are very much mistaken! (*To his wife, who has just entered.*) Come here for a minute, darling. I don't think I can take this much longer. (*Draws her aside, and from here on they talk in whispers.*) I haven't the faintest idea how much to pay this idiot for fixing that tap.

MRS. KISHON: How much does he want?

KISHON: "As much as you like." He's trying to be smart. I know his kind. All the same, what do you think? How much should I pay him?

MRS. KISHON: How long did he work?

KISHON: I know? I didn't check it with a stopwatch. Maybe half an hour. But that idiot also put in a washer.

STUCKS (*Whispers from the other side of the room.*): Two washers.

KISHON (*Goes on whispering.*): Yes. He put in two washers. And now who the hell knows how much you are supposed to pay?

MRS. KISHON: I think I know. If having your stockings repaired costs three shekels he can't ask more for fixing that tap than several times that.

KISHON: That's what I thought. The barber, for instance, takes ten shekels, but that's entirely different, he uses soap, but on the other hand, there is no washer, although of course the barber may cut with his razor if he isn't careful.

MRS. KISHON: I don't shave.

STUCKS (*Pulls out his watch, visibly impatient.*)

MRS. KISHON: I don't think the tap can be more than two or three times more expensive than a shave.

KISHON: Wait! (*To Stucks.*) Tell me, old boy, what's harder work for you, to shave or to fix a tap?

STUCKS: To fix a tap.

KISHON: Why?

STUCKS: Well, you see, shaving does not tire me, because with a good razor a weak beard like mine comes off easily. But such a four-inch tap needs a lot of handling.

MRS. KISHON (*Suddenly.*): Stop! I think I've got it! (*Draws Kishon aside and from here on they again talk in whispers.*) I know of a similar case. A few days ago they hauled a whole couch to the third floor for sixty shekels.

STUCKS (*Whispers.*): For seventy.

MRS. KISHON: All right, for seventy, what's the difference?

KISHON: Of course there is a difference. After all, we live on the second floor, and a tap is not nearly as heavy as a couch.

STUCKS: (*Again looks at his watch.*) It's getting late. I'm in a hurry.

KISHON: So who's keeping you? Why can't you make up your mind, damn it. How much you're going to ask?

STUCKS: Sorry, I thought that was what you were whispering about.

KISHON: Do you think we have nothing else to worry about than your few shekels? We thought all along that you were going to tell us how much we owe you.

MRS. KISHON: It's always the person who gets the money who had to name his price.

STUCKS: So that's all right, Mr. Kishon, you are a writer, you get lots of money. So please tell me the price.

KISHON: You are stubborn, aren't you? This is too ridiculous for words, so help me! All right, ten shekels? Twenty shekels? twenty shekels fifty? A hundred shekels? A thousand shekels?

STUCKS: Now, now, now, what's the matter with you, Mr. Kishon? A thousand shekels for fixing a tap? That's a lot of money for poor people like us. True, I put in two new washers, but I won't charge you for the filing, Mr. Kishon. I worked . . . (*Pulls out his watch*) All right, so pay me, Mr. Kishon – as much as you like.

KISHON: As much as I like? Listen carefully, old boy! You are not going to blackmail me. You may pull these tricks on people with weak nerves, but not on me! For me, to finish with people of your sort is as easy as this! (*Snaps his fingers.*) So for the last time: how much do I owe you?

STUCKS (*Also snaps his fingers.*): All right, let's see. I had two new washers . . . .

KISHON: You don't count the filing . . . .

STUCKS: Yes, now I do. (*Pulls out his watch.*) I fixed that tap, Mr. Kishon, very thoroughly . . . .

KISHON: Why do you keep looking at that miserable watch?

STUCKS: Why is it miserable?

KISHON: N-n-not miserable!

STUCKS: Then why say so? One has to watch one's language, Mr. Kishon!

KISHON (*In a hoarse whisper.*): Why do you keep looking at that watch?

STUCKS: Why do I keep looking at it? There are no hands on it anyway. I also took out its works, needs a bit of filing, you know. A complete filing job . . . .

KISHON: Is that so? (*Suddenly roaring.*) How much do I owe you?

STUCKS: Look, Mr. Kishon, so that we shouldn't quarrel, so that there should be no haggling, no argument . . . . (*Shakes hands with Kishon.*) Give me – as much as you like!

KISHON: Tell me, do you really want to kill me?

MRS. KISHON: Please, don't excite my husband!

STUCKS: Who's exciting him? Pardon me, ma'am, am I to blame if I'm so shy in business matters, not brash like other people?

KISHON (*Shouting.*): You are shy? You are a leech, that's what you are! Listen, old boy, do you really take me for a complete idiot?

STUCKS: No, no, I always exaggerate. Only yesterday I said so to my wife. We were in the park with my brother-in-law and little Hershele. (*The Kishons collapse into chairs, exasperated.*) Do you know little Hershele? A wonder kid, a real darling, the whole neighborhood is afraid of him. Well, to cut a long story short, let's not waste time, I'm in a hurry, I said to the wife just as we came to the first bench, I remember clearly, I said to the wife . . . or maybe we had already passed the first bench, I'm not quite sure, wait, let me think . . . . (*Walks up and down, trying to visualize their positions, mumbles to himself.*) We were standing here, so little Hershele came running this way . . . .

KISHON (*As if coming out of a trance.*): How much do I owe you?

STUCKS: Let's say it was just in front of the first bench, after all, the bench does not matter so much . . . .

KISHON (*Jumps at him, grabs him by the throat and shakes him.*): How much do I owe you?

STUCKS: I can't do it for less

KISHON (*Throttling him.*): How much do I owe you?

STUCKS (*Choking.*): As much as you can spare . . . for . . . this . . . .

MRS. KISHON (*Separates them with great difficulty, screaming.*): For God's sake, don't get so excited!

KISHON: You're right. This gangster is going to give me a heart attack. Here, old boy, take ten shekels and beat it! (*Drops into armchair and takes up paper, but his hands shake.*)

STUCKS (*Walks up to table with ponderous steps.*): What? Ten shekels. When the washers alone cost twelve? (*Bends over Kishon.*) Some people are stinking misers, dirty swine, miserable crooks . . . .

KISHON: Get out of here! (*Jumps up in a towering rage and throws Stucks' tool box, which had been standing on the table, to the ground. Ear-deafening crash. Tools scatter all over the room. Mrs. Kishon screams. Kishon drops, exhausted, into chair.*)

STUCKS: Say, what's going on here? (*Lifts his soldering lamp.*) Look, Mr. Kishon, now you broke my soldering lamp.

KISHON (*Utterly broken.*): All right, I'll pay. I'll pay for the washers, I'll pay for the filing, I'll pay for everything. How much do you get for the soldering lamp?

STUCKS (*Makes himself comfortable in the armchair, pulls out his watch.*): As much as you like, Mr. Kishon . . . .

Curtain

THE APOLLO MISSION

———□———

"**E**phraim," said the little woman, "Amir's in a mood." Preparations for the Purim Carnival were in full swing. Raphi was duly fixed up as a pirate with a slight touch of Military Police, but little Amir was sulking about the house with a face like thunder. Now and then he would aim a passing kick at the splendid costume that his mommy had made for him with her own hands. The fringed pants, the rubber boots, the ten-gallon hat, the gilded belt, and last but not least the stinking pistol – a complete outfit for the perfect cowboy – lay in a dark corner in utter *non grata*, while the *persona* himself was getting moodier by the moment.

"What's the matter, Amir?" we inquired at last. "Don't you want to be a cowboy?"

"No," said Amir, "I want to be an astronaut." He'd just been reading about Apollo 13 in his children's weekly.

"Pipe down," we told our son, "and we'll see what can be done."

"That's right," agreed the little woman, "we must talk it over and decide. . . ."

We held an impromptu parents' meeting and agreed that after all the kid's approach was not irrelevant: who *wouldn't* want to be an astronaut, mankind's spinning conscience? Gradually a compromise was hammered out.

"You be a cowboy just this time," we suggested to Amir, "and next year you can be an astronaut."

"No!" yelled our temperamental offspring. "Right now!"

"All right," we gave in with heavy heart. "So be an astronaut. We'll put a big pan on top of your head, and we'll write 'Apollo 13' on it in red paint. . . ."

"That's silly!" shrieks Amir fortissimo. "That's not an astronaut!"

"Then what is?"

"I don't know," sobs the child. "*You* ought to know!"

Why don't those guys fly to the moon *after* Purim? Is it too much to expect the U.S. Government to show some consideration for Israeli parents? Just listen to the kid's screams!

"Astro" – he screams – "nau-hau-haut!"

"All right," I say, "we'll stick a big mustache on your face."

"Don't want silly mustache! Astronautses don't have mustaches. . . ."

"A pair of glasses then!"

"Astronautses don't. . . ."

Damn thoughtless of them, I must say! How on earth can a responsible person fly to the moon without a mustache, without glasses, without any plainly recognizable mark of identification whatsoever?

"Got it!" I say. "Amir will put on Daddy's yellow pajamas. . . ."

"Don't want silly pajamas," howls the kid. "Wanna be a proper astronaut!"

"Let Daddy finish, will you? You'll wear my yellow pajamas and we'll stick a propeller in your botty. A real propeller that turns. . . ."

"Don't want silly poppeller!"

"Wings then. . . ."

"Not a silly bird! An astronaut!"

All that running about in space is nothing but a silly adventure, if you ask me!

"Daddy! Astro!"

The child nearly has a fit on the carpet. Only redheads can cry like that, back and forth and sideways with never a breath in between. Got to save him before he blows his little lungs.

"No problem at all," says Daddy. "Let's ring up Uncle Astronaut and ask him."

Amir falls incredibly silent, his blue eyes wide with hope. I pick up the phone and dial at random:

"Hallo, Apollo Headquarters?" I address the receiver. "Could I talk to the duty astronaut, please?"

"Who you wanting?" asks a woman at the other end of the line. "This Dr. Weisberger house."

"Hi Winston!" I exclaim joyfully. "How're things? Look, Amir wants to know how you're got up for your trip to the moon."

"Who?" – the woman again – "This Dr. Weisberger house."

"Hold on, Winston, I'll get a pencil," says Daddy.

"Now then, what do you say you're wearing? Fringed pants, rubber boots, ten-gallon hat. . . ."

"I not knowing Hebrew so good. Speak you German please?"

"Sure, I'm writing it down, Winston. Gilded belt and pistol. Fine, that's all I wanted to know. Give my regards to the President. . . ."

"Dr. Weisberger coming home in twelve."

"Thanks a lot."

I replace the receiver with a worried frown.

"Heard that?" I turn to Mommy. "Now where the hell are we going to get Amir all these things that astronauts wear?"

"Nuts!" shouts the idiot child dizzy with triumph. "They're there in the corner!"

That's how disaster was averted at the last moment with the aid of telecommunication. And if, dear reader, you should happen to see a very small cowboy with red hair about town these days, please cry out at the top of your voice: "Oho, there goes a real astronaut!" By the way, it's time they put a stop to those moon flights. They cost the earth.

□ *Tortures which the strongest man cannot endure are nowadays no longer the exclusive province of the secret police. They are now within easy grasp of the man in the street. All you need to practice them is a locked room, a bed, matches, a few garments, nylon stockings, various handbags, and your wife.*

THEY ARRIVED TOMORROW

—————□—————

"Ephraim," the wife shouted from the other room, "I'm almost ready."

The time was 9:30 P.M., the date December 31. The wife had been sitting in front of the wardrobe since sundown, preparing herself for the party at Tibi's in honor of the Gregorian New Year. I reminded her that we had promised our hosts to be there at ten o'clock, whereupon the little one said that it was quite all right to be fifteen minutes late, since the party would be boring at first in any case.

"All my dresses are old rags," the little one remarked, wearing a toga. "I haven't got a thing to wear."

I hear this remark every time we leave the house for any reason whatsoever, as if her wardrobe were not bursting with clothes. The idea behind the remark is to make me doubt my adequacy as a provider and in general to give me a nice inferiority complex. In fact, I don't understand a thing about her dresses; in my view they are all awful, and yet I always have to choose which dress she'll wear. Why?

"I've got that plain black dress," the little one ticked off the alternatives, "or the blue one with the high slit."

"That's it," I said, "the one with the slit."

"It's too solemn. How about the chemise?"

"Yes," I said. "That sounds good."

"But isn't it too sporty?"

"Sporty?" I scoffed. "What do you mean sporty?"

What, in fact, is a chemise? Only God knows. I closed her zipper and went to the bathroom for a shave while the wife changed her stockings for a more suitable color. After much searching, she found a proper stocking, but it had no mate. This is an elementary law: suitable stockings are always lonely in life. So now she had to take off her chemise and look for another rag better suited to the pearls she got for her last birthday from her husband's wife.

"It's ten," I alerted her while dressing hurriedly. "We'll be late!"

"Never mind," she says. "So you'll hear two off-color jokes less."

I was already in my festive trousers, but the wife was still puzzling over the question: pearls or silver brooch? The pearls are more decorative, but the brooch is more impressive.

It will be a miracle if we make it by eleven. I start reading the newspaper. The wife is looking for a belt to go with the silver brooch and is absolutely dejected: she has no suitable handbag to go with the new lacquered belt. I start writing a few letters, short stories, essays. . . .

"I'm ready," the wife shouts from the other room. "Come and do up my zipper."

I wonder what honest women would do about their zippers if their husbands escaped in good time? My guess is they wouldn't go to New Year parties. Nor are we going. The little one ties a small nylon apron around her neck and makes up her face. She applies the foundation that goes under the powder. The eyes are not yet touched up with mascara; they are still looking for shoes to go with the bag. The light pair happens to be at the shoemaker's, the black ones with the high heels are beautiful but you can't walk in them, in the low-heeled ones you can walk but they are low-heeled. . . .

"It's eleven!" I get up, fuming. "If you don't finish in a minute, I'll go by myself!"

"I'm ready," the wife calls from the other room. "You can't do the hully-gully anyway."

She takes off the little nylon apron because she has decided after all to wear the plain black dress. But where are the stockings to go with it? Where are the dark stockings? Eleven thirty.

I decide on a clever trick. I get up, walk with heavy steps to the entrance, shout a furious "Shalom," bang the door (as if I had left), and hold my breath as I hug the hall wall. . . .

Silence.

She has broken down apparently, the little one. A strong arm always helps. How did old man Nietzsche put it? "When going to a woman, don't forget the whip."

Five minutes go by in utter silence. It's a little uncomfortable to spend the rest of one's days in a dark hall. Perhaps something terrible has happened in that room. . . .

"Ephraim," the wife shouts, "come and do up my zipper!"

She has again slipped on the chemise (the plain black one has a burst sleeve seam). She has changed her stockings as well and is in a quandary over the pearls.

"Give me a hand, for goodness' sake," she says. "What do you suggest?"

I suggest we go to bed and have a good night's rest. Without another word I change into pajamas.

"Don't be ridiculous." The little one is furious. 'I'll be ready in ten minutes."

It's midnight. All over the country, chiming clocks are ushering in the New Year. Good night. I turn off the little bedside lamp and fall asleep. The last sight I remember was the wife bending down in front of the mirror, the nylon apron around her neck, tracing her eyebrows. I hate that little apron the way no little apron was ever hated. If I even think of it, my hand clenches in an iron fist. In my dream I was Charles Laughton, who as Henry VIII, it will be remembered, chopped off the heads of his six wives. Horrible mass scenes haunted my dreams. Women were carted off to the gallows while the crowds cheered. They changed stockings in the tumbril, smeared green paint around their eyes and one of them shampooed her hair and applied henna. . . .

After a deep and refreshing slumber of an hour and something I woke up next year. The wife was sitting in front of the mirror in the blue dress with the high slit, and was still painting her eyebrows with a black pencil, the tip of which she had burned with a match. A terrible weakness took hold of me.

"You know, old boy," my id whispered inside me in a completely indifferent voice, "you married a madwoman."

I looked at the watch: one fifteen. Id is right, this little woman is kookie. Suddenly the horrible thought flashed through my mind that I was in hell. As in Sartre's *No Exit*, the severest punishment of the sinner is to be locked in a small room with a woman who keeps dressing-dressing-dressing . . . forever!

As a matter of fact, I was a little afraid of her. Just then, she was moving all her little things from her big black handbag into the small black handbag. She was almost dressed – wait! – except for her hairdo. The big question was: to cover the forehead or leave it exposed? A few strands of hair make all the difference in the world.

"I'm ready," she announces, "get up!"

"Do you think it's still worth going?"

"What do you mean, is it worth going? Then why did I have to hurry. Don't worry, there'll be enough of those disgusting cocktail sausages left."

She was a little angry at me, I could feel it, because of my unconcealed impatience. The little apron was lying on the floor next to her. Quietly, I stretched out a foot, pulled it over with my toes and disappeared with it into the kitchen. I burned that apron with my own hands. I placed it in the sink and put a match to it, then watched the flames the way the Emperor Nero did in his time. It left an unpleasant smell, but I really had no choice. As I returned to the room, the little one was standing in front of the mirror in a quasi-finished state. I closed the zipper of the plain black dress and started dressing myself, hardly able to keep my eyes open, when – poof!

The run!

As I watched her from behind, I discovered . . . a run . . . in her left stocking . . . terrible! As the old Sanskrit proverb says: "Whoever changes stockings changes everything." Good Lord, let her not discover the run let her discover it only at the party if at all . . . after all, it's way back, the run Make a miracle, Almighty. . . .

I went quietly to my study and sat down at the desk.

"Don't waste time now," the wife shouted from the other room. "What are you doing there?"

"I am writing a scenario."

"I'm almost ready!"

"I know."

The work progressed nicely. I sketched in broad strokes the character of a great artist – a painter, violinist, humorist, what have you – who was expecting a great deal from life, but somehow got bogged down and was marking time, year after year. Why? Because of a woman, folks, who kept holding him back all the time. The writing proceeded with amazing ease. The artist realized his desperate plight and made up his mind to leave the woman who hampered him so grievously. On that long sleepless night he made a fateful decision. "Boy," he says to himself, "you'll get up and get the hell out of here."

Heavens!

The wife is in the bathroom washing her face. Two A.M. It's two o'clock. She finds the color of her eyelashes vulgar and puts on new makeup. For that you have to wash the face, service and grease it, the works. Everything from scratch. Utter despair grips me. Everything in the room seems to be mocking me. There is little sense in such a life. I walk over to the cupboard, take out a strong necktie and knot it to the top of the window. Let's finish and be done with it. . . .

The wife somehow senses that I am standing on a chair.

"Stop it, will you," she says, "and do up my zipper, please. What are you beefing about now?"

What am I beefing about? Good Lord, do I know what I'm beefing about at 2:30 in the morning, dressed in a shirt with a starched front and a dark jacket and striped pajama pants, while my little wife with one hand applies spray to her hair and with the other gropes in the closet for gloves? Gloves? It's hard to believe, but it looks as if this time she had really made it. A ray of hope stabs through the dismal darkness. So it has been worthwhile holding out. She is actually ready. In a little while we will go out and have a good time. Bursting with energy, the little one moves her little things from her small black handbag into her big black handbag and removes the pearls. I pull my dark trousers over the pajama pants. Everything is a little hazy. Outside dawn is breaking. Somewhere in Nazareth the church bells are ringing 3 A.M. in honor of the new Gregorian year. My nose is somewhat red because of the suppressed sobs. The little one remarks that I ought to perk up and, besides, I am stubble-faced – haven't I shaved?

"I did shave," I whisper, "long ago when you started dressing, I did shave." I go into the bathroom and with a trembling hand remove the three-o'clock shadow. I have lost my youth during this night. The face of a tortured old man is looking out at me from the mirror, the face of a man whom life has passed by. The face of a husband.

"I must always wait for you," the wife is carping in the other room. In the meantime she is looking for a suitable hat, because one of her locks is not sitting right. A last look in the mirror, a last dab at her face, a light brush of the powder which keeps falling . . . everything is fine . . . perhaps a little liquor is still left at Tibi's . . . are we going? Yes, let's . . .

The door opens. Impossible! We're off. We are off to the party.

"Wait!" The wife stops, thunderstruck. "There's a run in my left stocking!"

The rest is lost in the cosmic darkness from which there is no escape. The big zipper closed in on me. Inside the ghostly infinite, at a distance of millions of light years, there is music at the party – the party we never made.